A Lifetime Companion
to the Laws
of
Jewish Family Life

A LIFETIME COMPANION
TO THE LAWS
OF
JEWISH FAMILY LIFE

Deena R. Zimmerman
MD MPH IBCLC

Foreword by Rabbi Yehuda Henkin

URIM PUBLICATIONS
Jerusalem • New York

A Lifetime Companion to the Laws of Jewish Family Life
by Deena R. Zimmerman

Printed in Israel.
Third Revised Edition.
ISBN: 978-965-524-063-4

Urim Publications, P.O. Box 52287, Jerusalem 91521 Israel

Lambda Publishers Inc.
527 Empire Blvd.,
Brooklyn, New York 11225 U.S.A.
Tel: 718-972-5449 Fax: 718-972-6307
mh@ejudaica.com

www.UrimPublications.com

This book is dedicated to the memory of Moshe (Morris) Green *z"l*, the "Moshe" of Nishmat's Keren Ariel *Yoatzot Halacha* (Women Halachic Consultants) Program. Without his generosity, inspiration, energy and foresight, this program – which equipped me to write this book and, together with my colleagues on the program, to make an important contribution to Jewish life – would not have become the thriving reality that it is today.

דרש רבי שמלאי: מפני מה נתאוה משה רבינו ליכנס לארץ ישראל? וכי לאכול מפריה הוא צריך? או לשבוע מטובה הוא צריך? אלא כך אמר משה: הרבה מצות נצטוו ישראל ואין מתקיימין אלא בארץ ישראל, אכנס אני לארץ כדי שיתקיימו כולן על ידי. (תלמוד בבלי, סוטה יד.)

"Why did Moshe Rabbeinu want to go into the Land of Israel? Did he need to eat of its fruits or enjoy its bounty? Rather, Moshe said: Israel was commanded many commandments that can be observed only in the Land of Israel; let me enter the land so I can fulfill them." (*Babylonian Talmud, Sotah* 14a)

Moshe Green exemplified a similar attitude. He undertook his many philanthropic activities not for personal fame or benefit, but rather to increase the observance of the commandments. In recent years, he was especially committed to opening the highest reaches of Torah learning to women.

We are greatly saddened that he did not live to see the fruits of his labors, the graduation of the first *Yoatzot Halacha*.

CONTENTS

FOREWORD

by Rabbi Yehuda Henkin

Even more than Shabbat and kashrut, *taharat hamishpachah* serves as a yardstick by which commitment to Torah observance can be measured; there are those who fully observe the first two but not the latter, but rarely, if ever, the other way around. *Taharat hamishpachah* is unique in its centrality to married life, in its recurrently problematic nature and its pervasive influence on personal morals, and in its reliance on women. *"Vesafrah lah...,* She shall count seven days to herself" of a *zavah* is a mitzvah incumbent on the woman. She is in charge of counting, of checking herself, of noting and reporting her physical status, of bringing the requisite sacrifices to the Temple. Her husband is wholly dependent on her diligence and veracity.

This is all the more remarkable in view of the nature of the laws involved. Tractate *Niddah* is one of the three most difficult tractates in the Talmud. *Hilchot niddah* are intricate and complex, and mastery of them is a challenge even for the recognized scholar. At least a dozen compendiums of, and guides to, *hilchot niddah* have been written in the past forty years, in addition to a legion of codes, commentaries and responsa from previous generations. No two are the same; differences in rulings, in emphasis, and in authorities cited, are the norm. Yet the arena of *taharat hamishpachah* is the home and bedroom, far from the study-hall, and Rabbinic guidance is not always available when needed. This is true even today, and was certainly the case before telephones, faxes and email.

The ease with which *issur niddah* from the Torah can be violated and the grave consequences of doing so prompted protective rabbinical enactments as well as self-imposed *chumrot*, or stringencies. The classic example of the latter is the *"chumrah* of R. Zeira," by which any discovery of uterine blood necessitates the counting of seven blood-free days. During the course of centuries *chumrot* became normative and in turn produced new *chumrot*, following an inherent dynamic. This was only occasionally slowed by the countervailing argument, "would that Israel observe that which it has to [without burdening it with additional prohibitions]." The final arbiter was the community's willingness to accept *chumrot*, a willingness that can only be understood by reference to the fact that even inadvertent violation of God's law is intolerable. God's law in the Torah can be compared to His laws in nature: just as gravity makes one fall from a cliff regardless of what brought him to the edge, so, too, even the possibility of unintentional violation of Torah law justifies taking extreme precautionary measures. This approach – so foreign to modern prejudices, according to which subjectivity is sovereign and lack of intent can excuse anything – is firmly grounded in the Torah, which requires the bringing of sin-offerings for *inadvertent* violations. Recoil from even such a possibility is the essence of *yirat shamayim*, fear of heaven.

Some *chumrot* were adopted by entire Ashkenazi or Sephardi populations. Others, such as in the area of anticipated menses such as *veset Or Zarua* (twenty-four hours of separation rather than twelve), were adopted by some Jewish communities but not by others. This applies today to many areas of *hilchot niddah* and of Halacha in general. But it is a poor community or household indeed that, from off the shelves of Halacha, chooses only items bearing the lowest price-tag.

Nevertheless, there is no obligation to adopt stringencies when these are not dictated by heritage or community. Nor are all *chumrot* the same. Refraining from marital relations an additional *onah* or two a month will not harm anybody. The same cannot be said when separation is extended by a week, or more. For example, women, particularly in their forties, often have mid-cycle staining. This affects *shalom bayit*, and if it occurs regularly can eviscerate a marriage. There are few tensions like that of doing a *bedikah* in such circumstances. *Letaheir ishah leba'alah*, to enable a couple to resume relations, is a primary consideration, and in such cases Halacha cuts back on the number and nature of the *bedikot*.

This book is not intended to supplant membership in a specific community and the following of its customs and traditions, nor to preempt following the guidance of a local *rav*. Today, however, particularly since the destruction of the European communities, many if not most women lack an organic relationship with a community. They learn Judaism from books or in school, rather than via a mimetic relationship with their mothers and grandmothers. Particularly in the English-speaking communities, there has long been a need for an intelligently-written guide and introduction to *hilchot niddah*, a book which would fill the void between the overly-concise practical manuals and the extensive, scholarly expositions of the subject. Furthermore, reference to modern medical knowledge and techniques bearing on menstruation, contraception, etc., is essential.

Dr. Deena Zimmerman is uniquely qualified to write such a book. She is Jewishly learned, having twice completed the *daf yomi* cycle of the Talmud, part of which she taught in a daily *sheur.* She is a certified consultant in the field of *taharat hamishpachah,* one of the first graduates of the Keren Ariel *Yoatzot Halacha* program of Nishmat in Jerusalem. It was my pleasure to have been among the panel of rabbis who tested her upon completion of the program. In her work as a *yoetzet halacha,* she has had invaluable practical experience in addressing other women's questions and understanding their concerns. She is also a practicing physician (in pediatrics), and formerly an assistant professor in a medical school. She is, of course, a wife and a mother. The combination of knowledge and scholarship, experience, empathy and understanding she brings to this topic should help ensure **A Lifetime Companion to the Laws of Jewish Family Life** a place on the bookshelf of every modern woman committed to Halacha.

INTRODUCTION

The impetus for this book is simple. This is the type of book I would have wanted when I got married. There was no question about my keeping the laws of Jewish family life *(taharat hamishpachah)* – after all, I did my best to keep *Shabbat* and *Kashrut*, so why should these be any different? But unlike other areas of Jewish Law, this was one in which I had no prior experience or education. I needed to learn it from scratch, preferably with my husband to be. The problem was how to learn. The books available at the time had laundry lists of what to do and not do, but not placed in any framework that I could comprehend and thus retain. As for learning the *halachot* from the original sources, this was impossible within a four-month engagement while simultaneously attending medical school. Classes for brides and grooms of modern backgrounds did not exist. The classes that existed were, once again, listings of what to do and not to do, without sources and without much explanation. From lack of any alternative, I muddled through with the laundry lists.

For a decade and a half after getting married, I dreamed of writing this book. Although better pre-marital classes are currently available in some areas such as New York, they are not accessible to everyone. Furthermore, most classes are designed only for newlyweds, while these are *halachot* that apply during many years of married life. It would be helpful to have something in writing one could turn back to for a refresher course. I wanted such a book, but was not qualified to write it myself, and could not find anyone with sufficient knowledge of the *halachot* who wished to write it with me.

In 1997, Nishmat – the Jerusalem Center for Advanced Jewish Studies for Women – opened a program for studying these *halachot* on the intensive level that I had sought. The goal of Nishmat's "Keren Ariel" program is to train women to be an address for other women who have questions in this area of halacha but are hesitant to ask them. In the course of study, I further realized why I wanted this kind of book. Many laws that seemed difficult to keep, once explained and seen in the context of their original sources, made so much more sense. Often women do not understand the basics of these *halachot* even when they are fully committed to keeping them. This lack of knowledge leads to problems of both inappropriate leniency and unnecessary stringency.

After two years in the Keren Ariel program, I felt that I finally had the background to approach writing the book. Thanks to a post-graduate grant from Nishmat, this book has at last become a reality.

Why yet another book? How is this book different? First, especially in the first section of the book, many of the original sources of the *halachot* are provided in Hebrew. For those who grew up studying this way, this should be a welcome feature. For those for whom dealing with original Hebrew sources is difficult, the sections quoted are paraphrased in the following section.

Second, as this book is meant to be a lifetime companion, there are separate sections dealing with various stages of the life cycle. The laws of one's wedding night are usually relevant only once, while details about the peri-menopause are not interesting to most young brides. Third, this book contains detailed descriptions of medical situations in which questions in the area of *taharat hamishpachah* frequently arise.

The second section of the book is meant to be a quick practical review, as this is an area of halacha that frequently needs review. Months and sometimes years can go by with some of the laws being barely relevant, due to pregnancy and nursing, and thus subject to being forgotten. Alternatively, a woman may have a fairly regular cycle but as she gets older things change, leading to issues she never had to grapple with before. This section is also is a quick way to learn the laws if one does not have the time or inclination to study the sources provided in Part One.

This book cannot and is not meant to take the place of rabbinical consultation. Just as no medical manual can take the place of individual consultation with a physician, this book is not meant to take the place of a rabbi. Individual questions should be addressed to a couple's own rabbi, particularly as in many matters local practice is determinative of the halacha. However, if one does not understand the halachic issues involved, one often does not even know that a question can or should be asked.

Another reason to consult one's own rabbi is that some of the halachic opinions expressed here may not be those quoted in some other books – there are areas of disagreement in many areas of halacha. In addition, I do not claim to have listed all the details and sub-details of the *halachot*, which would be impossible even in a book of twice this size. Effort has been made, however, to widen the scope of debate in the footnotes, when possible.

The opinions expressed in the book have the approval of the rabbis whom I consulted, Rabbis Reuven Aberman, Yehuda Henkin and Yaakov Warhaftig. Responsibility for any errors that may have crept into this book, as well as for deciding what was included and what was omitted, is, of course, mine alone.

The focus of the book is on the Jewish laws of the physical relationship between the husband and wife. This is not meant in any way to negate the need for establishing and maintaining a healthy emotional relationship between the couple within the spirit of Judaism. Ideally, a couple will have personal guidance from a trusted advisor (e.g., rabbi, kallah teacher, parent) to help them on this path. If not, there are many books on this complementary topic. Preparation for Jewish family life should include addressing both issues.

This book is not for everyone. It includes clinical but explicit language about the human reproductive system that may make some people uncomfortable. This is not due to a lack of concern for the demands of modesty, but to prevent the confusion that too much euphemism can cause. Furthermore the book includes discussion of sensitive topics that are often not dealt with in texts. I feel these issues need to be dealt with openly, so people who find themselves in these situations know they are not alone.

For those people for whom this book *is* appropriate – I hope they enjoy the learning process of reading this book as much as I did the learning process of writing it.

Writing a book on halacha is an awesome task, as any misstatements can have serious ramifications. It is thus fitting that I end this introduction with the following:

רבי נחוניא בן הקנה היה מתפלל בכניסתו לבית המדרש וביציאתו תפלה קצרה.
אמרו לו: מה מקום לתפלה זו? אמר להם: בכניסתי אני מתפלל שלא יארע דבר
תקלה על ידי, וביציאתי אני נותן הודאה על חלקי. (תלמוד בבלי, ברכות כח:)

Rabbi Nechuniah ben Hakanah used to pray a short prayer when entering and leaving the house of study. They asked him: What is the purpose of this prayer? He told them: When I enter I pray that no problems should be caused by me, and when I leave I give thanks for my portion.
(Babylonian Talmud, *Berachot* 28b)

ACKNOWLEDGMENTS

First and foremost, I would like to thank my parents, Dr. Charles Cohen and Naomi Winter Cohen, for the Jewish education they gave me and for encouraging me to pursue it further. Similarly, I would like to thank the parents I acquired through my marriage, Morris and Elaine Zimmerman, who have provided me much love and support despite my somewhat unconventional pursuits. A thirst for advanced learning for women was something I also acquired from my grandmothers, Bess Winter and Sara Cohen of blessed memory.

I would also like to thank all my teachers through the years who have given me the skills to undertake such a project. Particular thanks (in chronological order) are due to my Ramaz School teachers – my first Talmud teacher, Rabbi Alan Odess, and my teacher and mentor through-out high school, Rabbi Jack Bieler. I thank Rabbi Yitzchak Frank who assisted me in continuing my Talmud studies after High School during my year in Israel, and tried to improve my Aramaic throughout the years. His insistence on excellence led him and his wife Marcia to read the manuscript and offer many helpful suggestions which I tried to incorporate. His concern for the benefit of the reader (as evidenced in his own book *The Practical Talmud Dictionary*) led him to offer to vocalize the Hebrew and Aramaic texts. Rabbi Reuven Aberman deserves special thanks for my first exposure to the systematic study of halacha. He also was an integral part of the production of the book, reviewing draft after draft and encouraging me to continue. Thanks as well to his wife Chaya for her tolerance of my many phone calls and visits.

This book owes its existence to the Keren Ariel Program for *Yoatzot Halacha* of Nishmat – the Jeanie Schottenstein Center for Advanced Torah Study for Women, in which I studied the laws of *taharat hamishpachah*, and a grant from which enabled me to write this book. Rabbanit Chana Henkin, Founder and Dean of Nishmat, conceived of the program and brought it into being. Moshe Green *z"l*, to whom the book is dedicated, was crucial to the inception of the program and of the post-graduate fellowships of which this book is the first fruit. His guidance is much missed. The ongoing support of his family and of my friends Ira and Michele Green have been crucial to the program's continued success. Rabbi Yaakov Warhaftig, dean of the program, took the brave step forward of teaching women on this level. He guided me during two years of intensive study, and continues to provide ongoing consultation in cases presented to me as a women's halachic advisor (*yoetzet halacha*). Rabbi Yehuda Henkin, Rav of Nishmat, thoroughly reviewed and corrected the manuscript and graciously agreed to write its forward.

Thanks for their thoughtful and careful review of draft copies go to my *chevrutah* Tova Ganzel and my colleagues from the Keren Ariel Program, Aliza Segal and Shani Taragin. Thanks for reviewing the manuscript also go to Dr. Yonina Schein, Dr. Roberta Colton, and Dr. Sharon Slater. Thanks for reviewing the medical sections to Dr. Gila Leiter and my brother Dr. Matthew Cohen. My thanks to Talli Y. Rosenbaum for her contribution of two appendices and of a number of helpful comments to the life cycle and medical sections. I wish to gratefully acknowledge the assistance of my publisher Tzvi Mauer both for his helpful comments and his efforts with the book's publication.

Much of the work on this book was done while working at TEREM – Immediate Medical Services, Jerusalem. I want to thank the doctors and nurses who work there with me and contributed their suggestions. I want to particularly express a debt of gratitude to the director, Rabbi Dr. David Applebaum *z"l*. At the time that I applied to the *yoetzet halacha* program, I was working at TEREM on the Sunday evening shift. This was the same evening that the medical lectures that were part of the program were given. Dr. Applebaum agreed to let me take a two hour break from my shift to attend these lectures as he felt that it was important that I be part of the program. He was fully aware of my writing this book at work and allowed me to do this "double duty." Dr. Applebaum was murdered in a terrorist attack in Jerusalem along with his daughter Naava, to whom I taught some of these *halachot*, on the evening before her wedding was to have taken place.

In writing this book I feel that I am partially filling a debt to my sister Dr. Jessica Cohen Langer and sister-in-law Dr. Sharon Koren Cohen who I taught about *taharat hamishpachah* prior to their respective weddings. At the time I felt that I never provided them with the type of education on the topic that they really deserved. I hope that this book will make it up to their daughters Ronit and Seela Langer and Atara, Tali and Tamar Cohen. My children Ari, Akiva, Yosef, Rivka and Tikva deserve many thanks for their patience so Ima could write her book. Most of all, none of my accomplishments would be possible without the support, encouragement and tolerance of my husband, Rabbi Sammy (Shalom) Zimmerman. May we merit bringing up our children together in health and happiness.

In the years since the first edition was published, a number of changes have taken place. First of all, Nishmat's Keren Ariel Program has expanded and matured. There are currently 60 certified *yoatzot halacha* serving communities in Israel and abroad. At present, *yoatzot halacha* answer questions nightly through Nishmat's Golda Koschitzky Women's Halachic Hotline (972-2-640-4343, or 1-877-YOETZET). I have had the privilege of developing Nishmat's Women's Health and Halacha Websites which include a site for the general public, www.yoatzot.org (including three online courses - Kallah Companion, Marriage Companion, and Spanish.*Taharat Hamishpajá*), and, for medical professionals, www.jewishwomenshealth.org. My work on the hotline and websites has given me exposure to over 10,000 questions in this area of halacha.

Secondly, while Torah is timeless, medicine is constantly changing. Thus there was a need to update a number of the medical issues discussed in this book.

I would like to thank Tzvi Mauer for his willingness to assure that each edition of this book is as accurate as possible. I would also like to thank Ilana Sober Elzufon for her painstaking work in indexing this book and her invaluable help in assuring that the writing of both revised editions (as well as anything posted on www.yoatzot.org) is as clear as possible.

The basic laws are presented twice.

Part ONE is meant as a study guide for those who wish to learn with the original sources. The sources in this part are in vocalized Hebrew; however, their content is paraphrased in the English paragraphs that follow each section.

Part TWO is for those who are interested primarily in knowing what to do, without sources, and for those who wish a shorter review.

Part THREE consists of a review of the life cycle with its attendant *halachot*.

Part FOUR deals with medical issues and their halachic implications.

PART ONE

THE STUDY GUIDE

Unlike many *halachot* which are taught at home and at school from a young age, the laws of *taharat hamishpachah* (family purity) generally are put off until shortly before marriage. At this exciting but hectic time of life, it is often difficult to learn, and much is soon forgotten. Furthermore, during extended periods of a married woman's life (such as pregnancy and breast-feeding), many normally basic laws do not apply, and it is easy to forget what one once knew. The goal of this book is to assist in learning the laws the first time, as well as to be a lifetime companion for refreshing one's knowledge.

CHAPTER 1

HILCHOT NIDDAH – BIBLICAL AND RABBINIC

The rules of *niddah* appear in the Torah twice.
The first is in Leviticus 15:19:

וְאִשָּׁה כִּי תִהְיֶה זָבָה דָּם יִהְיֶה זֹבָהּ בִּבְשָׂרָהּ שִׁבְעַת יָמִים תִּהְיֶה בְנִדָּתָהּ וְכָל הַנֹּגֵעַ בָּהּ
יִטְמָא עַד הָעָרֶב.

> A woman who has a flow of blood in her body shall be a *niddah* for seven days, and all who touch her shall be ritually impure until sundown.

Although many laws of ritual impurity do not apply today after the destruction of the Temple, the prohibition of sexual contact with a *niddah* still does. This is partially due to the fact that the prohibition of having sexual relations with a *niddah* also appears in Leviticus 18:19:

וְאֶל אִשָּׁה בְּנִדַּת טֻמְאָתָהּ לֹא תִקְרַב לְגַלּוֹת עֶרְוָתָהּ.

> A woman in the ritually impure state of *niddah*, you shall not approach for sexual relations.

In this source, *niddah* is included among forbidden sexual relationships (*arayot*) such as adultery and incest that remain in force at all times.

Niddah versus *zavah*

According to biblical law, uterine bleeding can cause a woman to assume either the status of *niddah*, the status of *zavah*, or the status of *yoledet* (*yoledet* will be discussed in Part Three, chapter 4), depending on when she bled and for how long. *Niddah* is the most common status, resulting from normal menses.

וְזֶה מִשְׁפָּטָהּ: מִשֶׁתִּרְאֶה טִיפַת דָּם אֲפִילוּ כְּחַרְדָּל אוֹ פָּחוֹת, בֵּין בְּאוֹנֶס בֵּין בְּרָצוֹן, מוֹנָה שִׁבְעַת יָמִים עִם יוֹם רְאִיָּיתָהּ וְטוֹבֶלֶת בְּלֵיל שְׁמִינִי. וְכָךְ הַדִּין: אֲפִילוּ שׁוֹפַעַת כָּל שִׁבְעָה, רַק שֶׁתִּפְסוֹק בְּטָהֳרָה בַּיּוֹם הַשְּׁבִיעִי קוֹדֶם בֵּין הַשְּׁמָשׁוֹת וּבְעֶרֶב טוֹבֶלֶת בְּלֵיל שְׁמִינִי. (טור ; יורה דעה, קפג)

A woman remains a *niddah* for seven days whether she bleeds for one day or the entire seven. Whenever the bleeding ceases, she ends her *niddah* status, according to original Torah law, immersing in the *mikveh* after nightfall of the seventh day – i.e., at the beginning of the eighth day.[1]

וּמִיּוֹם הַשְּׁבִיעִי וְאֵילָךְ עַד אַחַד עָשָׂר יוֹם, נִקְרָאִים יְמֵי זִיבָה, וְהֵן שֶׁהַחֲכָמִים קוֹרְאִין לָהֶם "אַחַד עָשָׂר יוֹם שֶׁבֵּין נִדָּה לְנִדָּה". וּמִשְׁפָּטָהּ בָּהֶן: אִם רָאֲתָה בָּהֶן יוֹם אֶחָד לְבַד – בֵּין שֶׁתִּרְאֶה בִּתְחִלַּת הַלַּיְלָה אוֹ בְּסוֹף הַיּוֹם, רַק שֶׁתִּפְסוֹק בְּטָהֳרָה – מְשַׁמֶּרֶת כָּל הַלַּיְלָה שֶׁאַחַר כָּךְ. אִם לֹא תִרְאֶה, תַּשְׁכִּים לְמָחָר וְתִטְבּוֹל מִיָּד מֵאַחַר הָנֵץ הַחַמָּה, אִם תִּרְצֶה; וּמִכָּל מָקוֹם אֲסוּרָה לְשַׁמֵּשׁ כָּל הַיּוֹם שֶׁמָּא תִּרְאֶה וְתִסְתּוֹר – וְזוֹ הִיא שֶׁנִּקְרֵאת "שׁוֹמֶרֶת יוֹם כְּנֶגֶד יוֹם". רָאֲתָה גַם בַּיּוֹם הַשֵּׁנִי וּפָסְקָה בּוֹ – מְשַׁכֶּמֶת בַּיּוֹם הַשְּׁלִישִׁי וְטוֹבֶלֶת, וְלֹא תְשַׁמֵּשׁ כָּל הַיּוֹם... וְגַם זוֹ בִּכְלַל שׁוֹמֶרֶת יוֹם כְּנֶגֶד יוֹם וְזוֹ הִיא שֶׁנִּקְרֵאת "זָבָה קְטַנָּה". (טור ; יורה דעה, קפג)

On the other hand, if a woman experiences uterine bleeding during the eleven days following the seven days of *niddah*, she acquires the status of *zavah*. One or two consecutive days of bleeding make her a *zavah ketanah* (minor *zavah*), and she has to wait until the following day (and is thus described שׁוֹמֶרֶת יוֹם כְּנֶגֶד יוֹם – i.e., keeping one day in the place of the other). On that following day, if she has discovered no additional blood during the night that passed, she can go to the *mikveh* anytime after sunrise.

---

[1] The Jewish day begins at sunset, with the day following the night, as the Torah states in Genesis 1: "and it was evening and it was morning."

רָאֲתָה גַּם בַּיּוֹם הַשְּׁלִישִׁי – נַעֲשֵׂית זָבָה גְדוֹלָה, וְלֹא תִטְהַר עַד שֶׁיִּהְיוּ לָהּ שִׁבְעָה יָמִים נְקִיִּים חוּץ מִיּוֹם שֶׁפּוֹסֶקֶת בּוֹ. וְטוֹבֶלֶת בַּיּוֹם הַשְּׁבִיעִי לְאַחַר הָנֵץ הַחַמָּה מִיָּד אֶלָּא שֶׁאֲסוּרָה לְשַׁמֵּשׁ שֶׁמָּא תִרְאֶה וְתִסְתּוֹר. (טור ; יורה דעה, קפג)

If the bleeding occurs on three or more consecutive days, the woman acquires the status of a *zavah gedolah* (major *zavah*), who needs to count seven blood-free days (*shiva neki'im*) before immersing in the *mikveh*.[2]

The *zavah ketanah* can go to *mikveh* anytime after sunrise on her blood-free day; similarly, the *zavah gedolah* may immerse after sunrise on her seventh blood-free day. However, neither one can resume relations with her husband until after nightfall, because she might discover blood later the same day. If that were to happen, the entire day retroactively would not be considered blood-free.

עָבְרָה כָּל אַחַד עָשָׂר יָמִים וְלֹא רָאֲתָה – חוֹזֶרֶת לִתְחִלַּת יְמֵי נִדּוּת. וְאִם רָאֲתָה בָּהֶם – נַעֲשָׂה זָבָה וְאֵינָהּ חוֹזֶרֶת לִימֵי הַנִּדּוּת עַד שֶׁיִּהְיוּ לָהּ שִׁבְעָה נְקִיִּים, וְאָז יַתְחִילוּ יְמֵי הַנִּדּוּת וְאַחֲרֵיהֶן יְמֵי הַזִּיבוּת. (טור ; יורה דעה, קפג)

Bleeding that occurs after the eleven "days of *zivah*" are over, renders a woman *niddah*. However, if she has become a *zavah gedolah*, she cannot revert to *niddah* status until seven blood-free days have passed.

These distinctions between *niddah* and *zavah* were of practical consequence only when these laws were observed on a biblical level. Today, a standard 11- or 12-day minimum separation period is in force, as will be explained.

Color of blood

דָּבָר תּוֹרָה חֲמִשָּׁה דָמִים טְמֵאִים בְּאִשָּׁה וְתוּ לָא. (טור ; יורה דעה, קפח)

---

[2] This is the method of counting according to the explanation of Rashi and most other authorities. The Rambam has a different method: from the time in her life that she is first a *niddah*, she continues to count seven days followed by eleven days consecutively and her status depends on which part of this cycle she experiences uterine bleeding. While the Rambam's method of calculation fits better with certain Talmudic passages, it is more difficult to explain its practical applications.

Another stipulation of biblical law is that only five forbidden colors of blood – four shades of red plus black – render a woman *niddah*.[3] Already in the time of the *Amoraim*, however, rabbis were hesitant to distinguish between the different colors.[4] Thus, it became accepted practice to forbid <u>all</u> shades of red and black. In the words of the *Tur*,

אֲבָל הָאִידְנָא, שֶׁנִּתְמַעֵט הַבְּקִיאוּת, חָזְרוּ לְטַמֵּאוֹת כָּל שֶׁיֵּשׁ בּוֹ מַרְאֵה אָדֹם, בֵּין אִם הוּא כֵּהֶה הַרְבֵּה אוֹ עָמוֹק, וְכֵן כָּל מַרְאֵה שָׁחוֹר. (טור ; יורה דעה, קפח)

This stringency, however, can lead to problems. A woman might start counting the seven days of *niddah* as a result of experiencing a discharge she thought was of a forbidden color, but which was actually a permissible one. If a few days later she discovered blood of a forbidden color, she might end the seven days too early by having started to count from the initial discharge. She might become confused about whether she was in her days of *niddah* or her days of *zivah*. In the words of the *Tur*,

מִשֶּׁרַבּוּ הַגָּלֻיּוֹת וְתָכְפוּ הַצָּרוֹת וְנִתְמַעֲטוּ הַלְּבָבוֹת, חָשׁוּ שֶׁמָּא יָבֹאוּ לִטְעוֹת בְּאִיסּוּר כָּרֵת – שֶׁמָּא תִּרְאֶה אִשָּׁה בִּימֵי נִדָּתָהּ שִׁשָּׁה יָמִים וְיִהְיֶה הַכֹּל דָּם טוֹהַר, וּבַשְּׁבִיעִי תִּרְאֶה דָּם טָמֵא וּסְבוּרָה לִטְבֹּל בְּלֵיל שְׁמִינִי וּצְרִיכָה עוֹד שִׁבְעָה יָמִים – הֶחְמִירוּ לְטַמֵּא כָּל מַרְאֵה דָּם אָדֹם ; וּכְדֵי שֶׁלֹּא יָבֹאוּ לִידֵי טָעוּת בֵּין יְמֵי נִדָּה וִימֵי זִיבָה, הוֹסִיפוּ חֻמְרָא אַחַר חֻמְרָא עַד שֶׁאָמְרוּ שֶׁאֲפִילּוּ אִם לֹא תִרְאֶה אֶלָּא טִיפַּת דָּם כְּחַרְדָּל תֵּשֵׁב עָלֶיהָ שִׁבְעָה נְקִיִּים כְּזָבָה גְדוֹלָה. (טור ; יורה דעה, קפג)

To solve the above mentioned problems, Rabbi Yehudah Hanasi decreed: if a woman bled on one or two consecutive days she should count six blood-free days; if she bled on three days she should count seven blood-free days. In this way, all contingencies were covered. However, women apparently found this confusing and thus took it upon themselves to wait seven blood-free days after any bleeding at all. This is the halacha today: after any bleeding that renders a woman impure, she has to count seven blood-free days as if she were a *zavah gedolah*. Furthermore, in most

---

[3] *Niddah* 19a lists the red of blood from a laceration, black, the red of the saffron flower, the red of water mixed with the dirt from the valley of *Bet Kerem* and the red of diluted wine.

[4] *Niddah* 20b.

situations, she cannot begin to count these seven days until a minimum of 4 or 5 days[5] have passed from the onset of her *niddah* status, for reasons that will be discussed below.

While the counting of these seven days is often referred to as the "*chumrah* (stringency) of Rabbi Zeira,"[6] it has been so assimilated into halachic practice that it is cited as the classic example of "*halacha pesukah,*" a ruling that all agree to. While certain rabbinic decrees in *hilchot niddah* are occasionally treated leniently, this regulation is almost never dispensed with.

---

[5] Many Sephardi women wait four days, while the Ashkenzi practice is to wait five days. The need for a minimum of days before starting to count *shiva neki'im* is discussed in depth in chapter 3 (pp.45-46).

[6] This progression is recorded in the *Babylonian Talmud* in *Niddah* 66a. The phrase חומרא דרבי זירא first appears in the *Tosephot* in a number of locations including *Niddah* 67b.

CHAPTER 2

THE ONSET OF THE *NIDDAH* STATUS

Bleeding

"וְאִשָּׁה כִּי תִהְיֶה זָבָה, דָּם יִהְיֶה זֹבָהּ בִּבְשָׂרָהּ, שִׁבְעַת יָמִים תִּהְיֶה בְנִדָּתָהּ" (ויקרא
טו:יט) וְלָמְדוּ חֲכָמִים מִמִּדְרַשׁ הַפְּסוּקִים, שֶׁלֹּא בְכָל מָקוֹם שֶׁתָּזוּב מִמֶּנָּה דָם טְמֵאָה,
אֶלָּא דַוְקָא דָם הַבָּא מִן הַמָּקוֹר. (טור ; יורה דעה, קפג)

> "A woman who has a flow of blood in her body shall be a
> *niddah* for seven days" (Leviticus 15:19). The Sages derived
> through exegesis of this verse that she does not become im-
> pure from blood that flows from any part of her body, but
> specifically from blood that comes from the uterus (the *ma-
> kor*, lit. "source"). (*Tur, Yoreh Deah* 183)

Thus, bleeding not from a uterine source, such as from a vaginal
laceration, does not make one a *niddah*. Similarly, any other bleeding in the
genital/rectal area, such as from hemorrhoids, does not make a woman a
niddah.

> וְלֹא כָל דָּם הַבָּא מִן הַמָּקוֹר טָמֵא אֶלָּא דַוְקָא חֲמִשָּׁה מִינֵי דָמִים....
> (טור ; יורה דעה, קפג)

אֲבָל הָאִידָנָא שֶׁנִּתְמַעֵט הַבְּקִיאוּת חָזְרוּ לְטַמְּאוֹת כָּל שֶׁיֵּשׁ בּוֹ מַרְאֶה אָדוֹם בֵּין אִם
הוּא כֵּהֶה הַרְבֵּה אוֹ עָמוֹק, וְכֵן כָּל מַרְאֶה שָׁחוֹר ; וְאֵין טָהוֹר אֶלָּא בִּשְׁנֵי מַרְאוֹת שֶׁהֵן
הַלָּבָן וְהַיָּרוֹק בֵּין יָרֹק כְּכַרְתֵּי בֵּין צָהוֹב כְּזָהָב, אֲפִילּוּ אִם יֵשׁ בּוֹ סְמִיכוּת דָּם וְהוּא עָב
הַרְבֵּה. (טור ; יורה דעה, קפח)

As mentioned above, at the time of the giving of the Torah, only discharge of five specific shades of red and black rendered a woman *niddah*. By the Talmudic period, however, a number of authorities no longer felt that they could differentiate between similar shades of red.[1] Over time, all reds became forbidden. Other colors of uterine discharge such as white (physiologic leukorrhea) and green are completely permissible. Light yellow does not render her a *niddah*, but deeper hues of yellow may be problematic. Oranges and browns need to be shown to an authority to determine if they are too close to red.[2] All questionable colors should be shown to an authority and should not automatically be assumed to be prohibited or permitted.

וְאַף בָּאֵלוּ אֵינָה טְמֵאָה עַד שֶׁתַּרְגִּיש בִּיְצִיאָתוֹ. (טור; יורה דעה, קפג)

Even when there is red uterine bleeding, according to biblical law she is not a *niddah* until she "feels," i.e., she has a bodily sensation (*harga-shah*) that accompanies the blood's exit.[3] The Talmud does not spell out what exactly this sensation is; apparently it can be rather strong, since the Talmud speaks of it awakening her at night.[4] Later sources describe three forms of sensation:

---

[1] *Niddah* 20b

[2] This is an area of *hilchot niddah* that makes many women very uncomfortable – see Frequently Asked Questions at the end of Part Two.

[3] *Niddah* 57b

אָמַר שְׁמוּאֵל: בָּדְקָה קַרְקַע עוֹלָם וְיָשְׁבָה עָלֶיהָ, וּמָצְאָה דָם עָלֶיהָ – טְהוֹרָה, שֶׁנֶּאֱמַר "בִּבְשָׂרָה" – עַד שֶׁתַּרְגִּיש בִּבְשָׂרָה.

Shmuel states that even if she previously checked the ground on which she sat and found no stain, and upon rising found blood, in the absence of sensation, she would not be *niddah*.

[4] *Niddah* 3a

יְשֵׁנָה נַמִי, אַגַּב צַעֲרָה מִיתְּעָרָא.

If she was asleep, the pain would have awakened her.

1. Her whole body shakes.[5]

2. She feels her uterus open.[6]

3. She feels liquid flowing.[7]

About this last sensation, there is disagreement between the authorities as to a) whether it is a halachically relevant sensation at all[8] and b) if so, where in the reproductive system she needs to feel flow in order for it to have halachic implications.[9]

Blood found in or exiting from the vaginal canal in the absence of these sensations does not render a woman a *niddah* by biblical law. Howev-

---

[5] Rambam, *Isurei Biah* 5:17

וַאֲפִילוּ הִרְגִּישׁ גּוּפָהּ וְנִזְדַּעְזְעָה.

[6] *Pitchei Teshuvah* 183:1 lists all three sensations:

וְדַע דְּשְׁלֹשָׁה מִינֵי הַרְגָּשׁוֹת יֵשׁ לְעִנְיַן שֶׁתְּהֵא טְמֵאָה מִדְּאוֹרָיְיתָא

א׳ שֶׁנִּזְדַּעְזַע גּוּפָהּ

ב׳ שֶׁנִּפְתַּח מְקוֹרָהּ

ג׳ שֶׁדָּבָר לַח זָב מִמֶּנָּה בִּפְנִים.

[7] *Noda Beyehudah, Mahadurah Kama,* YD 55

נִרְאֶה לְעַנְיוֹת דַּעְתִּי דְּאַף הַרְגָּשַׁת זִיבַת דָּבָר לַח חָשִׁיב הַרְגָּשָׁה, וְלֹא בָּעִינַן הַרְגָּשַׁת פְּתִיחַת הַמָּקוֹר.

The *Aruch Hashulchan Yore Deah* 183 describes it as a small pain.

[8] The *Noda Beyehudah* (above) and the *Chavot Daat* (YD 190:1) consider this a relevant sensation. The *Chatam Sofer* [YD 145, 153, 167, 171] does not. General practice follows the first opinion but it is important to inquire which sensation a woman experienced, as in some cases this can be relevant.

[9] The *Noda Beyehudah* and *Chavot Daat* disagree as to whether it is only flow from the uterus to the vaginal canal, or also flow within the vaginal canal itself. Some modern authorities contend that, as most women cannot make such fine differentiations, when a women feels only an external flow (i.e., from the vagina to the outside), we must suspect that perhaps she actually felt an internal flow (*Igrot Moshe* YD 4:17[7]). A feeling of external dampness, however, is NOT a *hargashah*, and neither are sensations such as backache, abdominal cramps, or bloating. The latter will be discussed under *Veset Haguf* (p. 70).

er, since there may have indeed been a sensation of which she did not take note, she is a *niddah* according to rabbinic law.

There are also circumstances, all involving the genital area, in which we are particularly concerned that she may have experienced a sensation but overlooked it or attributed it to something else:

1. Urination

2. Sexual intercourse

3. Internal examination (*bedikah*).

Therefore, if a woman sees blood immediately[10] after urination or intercourse, or finds blood on the cloth she used for an internal examination, the laws are stringent because she may have had a sensation (making her *niddah* by biblical law) of which she was not aware.[11]

If a woman definitely did have a sensation – a relatively rare occurrence for most women – she should do an internal examination (how to do this will be discussed on pp. 40–41). If she finds a forbidden color, she becomes a *niddah*. If she finds only a discharge of a permissible color, however, she can attribute the sensation to that discharge and is still permitted to her husband. If she does not find anything she should consult a rabbi, as there are situations that would make her *niddah*, and others that would leave her permitted.[12]

---

[10] The time period is described in the Talmud (*Niddah* 12a) as tiny, that "immediately after the penis exits, the *bedikah* cloth enters." The *Shulchan Aruch* 187:1 describes a somewhat longer period, the time it would take her to put her hand under her pillow, take a cloth from there and wipe herself. This is also a very short time. For practical purposes, estimates are 10–15 seconds.

[11] Inserting a tampon or diaphragm may have the same implications. See *Igrot Moshe* YD 4:17 [16].

[12] *Yabia Omer*, 5 YD 15.

Stains

דְּבַר תּוֹרָה אֵין הָאִשָּׁה מִטַּמְּאָה וְלֹא אֲסוּרָה לְבַעְלָהּ עַד שֶׁתַּרְגִּישׁ שֶׁיָּצָא דָם מִבְּשָׂרָהּ, וְחֲכָמִים גָּזְרוּ עַל כָּל כֶּתֶם שֶׁנִּמְצָא בְגוּפָהּ אוֹ בְּבִגְדֶיהָ שֶׁהִיא טְמֵאָה וַאֲסוּרָה לְבַעְלָהּ אֲפִילּוּ שֶׁלֹּא הִרְגִּישָׁה וַאֲפִילּוּ בָדְקָה עַצְמָהּ וּמְצָאָהּ טְהוֹרָה. (טוּר; יוֹרֶה דֵּעָה, קצ)

As mentioned above, according to biblical law a woman does not become a *niddah* unless she experienced a sensation (*hargashah*). If she merely found a bloodstain on her clothing she would not be a *niddah* as regards marital relations. On the other hand, the clothing itself would be ritually impure as regards contact with sanctified objects, because the bloodstain might have come from a *niddah*. As this situation was rather anomalous, the rabbis decreed that if she found a bloodstain on her clothes or body she would have the status of *niddah*, and observe all its laws, even if she did not experience a sensation.[13]

לֹא גָזְרוּ עַל הַכֶּתֶם אֶלָּא אִם כֵּן יְהֵא בּוֹ 'כִּגְרִיס וָעוֹד', וּגְרִיס הוּא תֵּשַׁע עֲדָשׁוֹת, שֶׁכָּל זְמַן שֶׁאֵין בּוֹ כָּזֶה הַשִּׁיעוּר אָנוּ תּוֹלִין לוֹמַר דַּם כִּנָּה הוּא. (טוּר; יוֹרֶה דֵּעָה, קצ)

When the rabbis decreed that bloodstains (*ketamim*) make a woman *niddah* even without *hargashah*, they included a number of conditions so that couples would not be constantly prohibited from having sexual relations:

1. Size: If the stain (*ketem*) is less than the size of a *gris*[14] [see Figure on next page], it does not count. From a halachic standpoint, this blood can be

---

[13] *Chatam Sofer* YD:150

מִשּׁוּם דְּתִחְלַּת גְּזֵירַת כֶּתֶם הָיָה מִשּׁוּם חוּמְרָא דְטָהֳרוֹת,... וְלָא פְּלוּג רַבָּנָן וְטִמְּאוּ אוֹתָהּ גַּם לְבַעְלָהּ שֶׁלֹּא תִּהְיֶה חוּכָא: הָאִשָּׁה טְמֵאָה נִדָּה לְטָהֳרוֹת וּטְהוֹרָה לְבַעְלָהּ וְכֵיוָן שֶׁנֶּאֱסַר בְּמִנְיָן, אִם כֵּן אַף עַל פִּי שֶׁבָּטֵל טַעַם טָהֳרוֹת, מִכָּל מָקוֹם גְּזֵרָה לֹא בָּטְלָה וַעֲדַיִין אֲסוּרָה לְבַעְלָהּ.

[14] Literally, this is a split granule of grain or pulse. This refers to a measure that is the area exposed when such a granule is split in half. This, by most opinions, represents a circle whose diameter is 19 mm (approximately 3/4 of an inch). For further discussion, see the appendix of Frank, Y. *The Practical Talmud Dictionary*, Second Edition (Jerusalem: Ariel Institute, 1994).

attributed to a louse, even though body lice that contain so much blood are not common today.[15]

אִם אֵין בְּכֻתֶם אֶחָד בְּמָקוֹם אֶחָד כִּגְרִיס אַף עַל פִּי שֶׁיֵּשׁ טִיפִּין הַרְבֵּה סְמוּכִין זֶה לָזֶה עַד שֶׁאִם נְצָרְפֵם יֵשׁ בָּהֶן יוֹתֵר מִכִּגְרִיס – טְהוֹרָה, שֶׁאָנוּ תוֹלִין כָּל טִיפָּה וְטִיפָּה בְּכִינָה עַד שֶׁיְּהֵא בּוֹ כִּגְרִיס וְעוֹד בְּמָקוֹם אֶחָד. בַּמֶּה דְבָרִים אֲמוּרִים? כְּשֶׁהַטִּיפִּין עַל חֲלוּקָה – אֲבָל אִם הֵם עַל בְּשָׂרָהּ, מִצְטָרְפִין לְכִגְרִיס. (טור; יורה דעה, קצ)

If she has a number of small stains, if they are on clothing, then each one is judged separately. If they are on her body, then one adds the total surface area of the stains; if together they comprise more than a *gris*,[16] in the absence of other mitigating factors, she is a *niddah*.

2. Type of surface: A stain that is found on something not halachically susceptible to ritual impurity does not make a woman *niddah*, as stated below:

כֶּתֶם שֶׁנִּמְצָא עַל דָּבָר שֶׁאֵינוֹ מְקַבֵּל טוּמְאָה לֹא גָזְרוּ עָלָיו. כֵּיצַד? בְּדְקָה קַרְקַע עוֹלָם... אוֹ כָּל דָּבָר שֶׁאֵינוֹ מְקַבֵּל טוּמְאָה וְיָשְׁבָה עָלָיו וּמָצְאָה בּוֹ כֶּתֶם – טְהוֹרָה. (טור; יורה דעה, קצ)

---

[15] The *Chatam Sofer* YD 2:150 explains that even though today it is unlikely that a louse would cause that size bloodstain, it is still the size that applies currently. His reasoning is that originally the decree of stains was related to issues of ritual impurity which are currently not in force. Even though we still need to observe the rabbinic decree, we only need do so in its minimal original form.

וְכֵיוָן שֶׁכָּל עַצְמָהּ לֹא נֶאֶסְרָה לְבַעֲלָהּ אֶלָּא מִתַּקָּנַת חֲכָמִים הָרִאשׁוֹנִים, אִם כֵּן אֵין לָנוּ לְטַמְּאוֹתָהּ אֶלָּא בְּשִׁעוּר כֶּתֶם שֶׁבִּזְמַנֵּיהֶם שֶׁהָיָה מַאֲכֹלֶת גְּדוֹלוֹת מְצוּיוֹת אַף עַל פִּי שֶׁבִּזְמַנֵּינוּ אֵין נִמְצָא כָזֹאת.

[16] This is the opinion of most authorities. A minority view is stringent concerning blood of any size found on the body (*Shulchan Aruch Harav*). See: Rav Yekutiel Farkas. *Taharah Kehalacha* [heb]. *Torat Chaim* 5758 p. 19.

Stains on this type of surface were excluded from the rabbinic decree of *ketamim* as the original reason for the decree related to the ritual impurity of sanctified objects, as explained above. Common examples are a plastic toilet seat, the ground and, according to many opinions, toilet paper.[17] Blood found on stool is also permissible for this reason.[18]

3. Color of the garment:

וְכֶתֶם הַנִּמְצָא עַל בֶּגֶד צָבוּעַ – פְּלִיגִי בַּהּ : תַּנָּא קַמָּא מְטַמֵּא וְרַבִּי יוֹנָתָן מְטַהֵר. וּפָסַק הָרַמְבַּ"ן כְּתַנָּא קַמָּא, וְהָרַמְבַּ"ם כְּרַבִּי יוֹנָתָן. וְכָתַב אֲדוֹנִי אָבִי הָרא"ש ז"ל : וּבִכְתָמִים שׁוֹמְעִין לְהָקֵל. (טור ; יורה דעה, קצ)

If a stain is found on a colored surface,[19] it does not count. There is a difference of opinion on this; however, since stains are only a rabbinical decree, we follow the more lenient opinion.

4. Location:

לֹא בְּכָל הַמְּקוֹמוֹת שֶׁיִּמָּצֵא שָׁם כֶּתֶם טָמֵא, אֶלָּא דַוְקָא בְּמָקוֹם שֶׁאֶפְשָׁר שֶׁבָּא שָׁם מִן הַמָּקוֹר. (טור ; יורה דעה, קצ)

Only stains found in places where they could conceivably have come from the uterus render her a *niddah*. Thus stains on her legs are problematic, but those on her upper arms are not, unless she had done handstands or other acrobatics.

---

[17] See Frequently Asked Questions at the end of Part Two (p. 102) for further discussion of toilet paper.

[18] The bleeding is also most likely to be from a rectal source, e.g., hemorrhoids.

[19] Colored surfaces include even light colors, where one can see that there is a stain but can no longer tell its exact hue. Different shades of white, however, are considered as white. Whether beige is considered dark white (uncolored) or light brown (colored) is a matter of debate, and one should consult one's rabbi.

5. Other logical explanation. For example:

> a. If she has a wound in her body from where the blood could have come, she can ascribe the stain to that wound, and she is not a *niddah*.

אִם יֵשׁ בָּהּ מַכָּה בְּגוּפָהּ, שֶׁיְּכוֹלָה לִתְלוֹת בָּהּ שֶׁאֶפְשָׁר שֶׁיָּבֹא הַדָּם מִמֶּנָּה, תּוֹלָה בָּהּ
וּטְהוֹרָה. (טוּר ; יוֹרה דעה, קצ)

> b. If she was working with blood, such as drawing blood in a laboratory, suturing a wound, or cleaning chickens, she can ascribe the stain to her work, and she is not a *niddah*.

כָּתַב הָרַמְבַּ"ן שֶׁתּוֹלָה בְּכָל מַה שֶׁיֵּשׁ לִתְלוֹת, כְּגוֹן שֶׁנִּתְעַסְּקָה בִּכְתָמִים אוֹ עָבְרָה בְּשׁוּק
שֶׁל טַבָּחִים – תּוֹלִין וּטְהוֹרָה. (טוּר ; יוֹרה דעה, קצ)

> c. If she can attribute the blood she found to someone else, such as if she had lifted a child with a nosebleed, she can ascribe the stain to that person, and she is not a *niddah*.

וּכְשֵׁם שֶׁתּוֹלָה בָּהּ, כָּךְ תּוֹלָה בְּבַעֲלָהּ וּבִבְנָהּ אִם נִתְעַסְּקוּ בִּכְתָמִים אוֹ אִם יֵשׁ בָּהֶם
מַכָּה, לְפִי שֶׁדַּרְכָּן לִיגַּע בָּהּ. (טוּר ; יוֹרה דעה, קצ)

The rules for assuming that the stain is due to external causes are somewhat more stringent during the first three days of the seven blood free days. Thus, if she is not absolutely sure that the stains found during those days are from an external source, she should consult a rabbi.

When she experiences a sensation

When she did experience a halachically relevant sensation, (as described above) the principles concerning stains found subsequently are more stringent:

1. There is no minimum size[20] – even a pinprick of blood makes her a *niddah*.

2. The stain cannot be attributed to other causes.

וּמִיהוּ מִשֶּׁתַּרְגִּישׁ בּוֹ שֶׁנֶּעֱקַר מִמְּקוֹמוֹ וְיָצָא לְבֵית הַחִיצוֹן – טְמֵאָה וְאַף עַל פִּי שֶׁלֹּא יָצָא לַחוּץ. (טור ; יורה דעה, קפג)

If she did have a halachically relevant sensation, she becomes a *niddah* from the point in time that blood reaches the vagina, even if it has not yet exited her body. Due to this, it is very important that she check herself internally on certain occasions[21] as will be discussed below.

When she states she is a *niddah*

The woman is the one who informs her husband of her status. Therefore, her words are important and bear halachic standing.

הָאִשָּׁה שֶׁהִיא בְּחֶזְקַת טְמֵאָה, אָסוּר לוֹ לָבֹא עָלֶיהָ עַד שֶׁתֹּאמַר לוֹ : טָבַלְתִּי. (שולחן ערוך ; יורה דעה, קפה:א)

אָמְרָה לְבַעְלָהּ : טְמֵאָה אֲנִי, וְאַחַר כָּךְ אָמְרָה : טְהוֹרָה אֲנִי, אֵינָהּ נֶאֱמֶנֶת. (שם ; סעיף ג)

Her words have so much halachic import, that if she <u>states</u> she is a *niddah* she is considered as one. Furthermore, even if she first states she is a *niddah* and then states that she is not, she is still considered a *niddah* and has to

---

[20] Although the phrase is "as small as a mustard seed," this is taken to mean any size, even if smaller.

[21] On the other hand, she does not have to do internal exams at other times. While sources such as *Mishna Niddah* 2:1 mention that

היד המרבה לבדוק בנשים משובחת

this applies to the time when people ate food in a status of *taharah*. When women do excessive internal exams, especially at times in their cycle when they have less natural lubrication, they are liable to abrade the vaginal lining and cause unnecessary problems.

count the requisite days and immerse in the *mikveh* even though she may have had no bleeding at all. The only exception to this last situation is if she has a good explanation for why she misspoke. Some examples of acceptable excuses are:

1. She was embarrassed by her husband's attentions in the presence of other people.

2. She wished to deter her husband's advances, as she did not feel well.

3. She thought she was in fact *niddah*, but on consultation with a rabbi found out that she was not.[22]

Childbirth (see also separate chapter in Part Three, pp.127–132)

יוֹלֶדֶת, אֲפִילוּ לֹא רָאֲתָה דָם, טְמֵאָה כְּנִדָּה – בֵּין יָלְדָה חַי, בֵּין יָלְדָה מֵת וַאֲפִילוּ נֵפֶל. וְכַמָּה הֵם יְמֵי טוּמְאָתָהּ? עַכְשָׁיו בַּזְּמַן הַזֶּה כָּל הַיּוֹלְדוֹת חֲשׁוּבוֹת יוֹלְדוֹת בְּזוֹב וּצְרִיכוֹת לִסְפּוֹר שִׁבְעָה נְקִיִּים. (שלחן ערוך ; יורה דעה, קצד:א)

By biblical law, a woman had the status of *yoledet*, whose laws are analogous to those of *niddah*, for one week after the birth of a son and two weeks after the birth of a daughter. This was true whether she experienced bleeding or not because it is halachically assumed that with any opening of the uterus some blood has exited, as will be discussed in a later chapter (pp.127–128). According to biblical law, starting with day eight for a boy or day fifteen for a girl, uterine bleeding assumed a different status – that of *dam tohar*. This status lasted for 33 days for a boy and 66 days for a girl. While experiencing *dam tohar*, the woman was permitted to have marital relations with her husband, but was not yet sufficiently *tehorah* (ritually pure) to bring sacrifices to the Temple.

Today, however, according to rabbinic law, we consider all women who give birth, or have a miscarriage more than 40 days after conception,

---

[22] In general, to avoid problems, if a wife is not sure that she is a *niddah* she should tell her husband that she is not sure. While the couple needs to keep the laws of the *niddah* status during the time of uncertainty, this maintains the element of doubt.

as if they had given birth while in the status of *zavah*. Thus the woman has the status both of *zavah* and *yoledet*, and needs to count seven blood-free days (*shiva neki'im*) before she can immerse in the *mikveh*. This need for the *shiva neki'im* applies both to the bleeding that accompanies childbirth and to any further bleeding thereafter, even within the 33/66 day time period.

Bride (see also separate chapter in Part Three, pp. 123–124)

הַכּוֹנֵס אֶת הַבְּתוּלָה, בּוֹעֵל בְּעִילַת מִצְוָה וְגוֹמֵר בִּיאָתוֹ וּפוֹרֵשׁ מִיָּד... וּצְרִיכָה שֶׁתִּפְסוֹק בְּטׇהֳרָה וְתִבְדּוֹק כָּל שִׁבְעָה, וְלֹא תַּתְחִיל לִמְנוֹת עַד יוֹם חֲמִישִׁי לְשִׁימוּשָׁהּ. וְנוֹהֵג עִמָּהּ כְּכָל דִּינֵי נִדָּה לְעִנְיַן הַרְחָקָה. (שולחן ערוך ; יורה דעה, קצג:א)

Although bleeding that may accompany the stretching of the hymen the first time a woman has intercourse is NOT uterine bleeding, the woman has the status of *niddah* by rabbinic decree. When the wife is a virgin, the couple can complete the first act of intercourse after the wedding, but then, even if she does not see any blood, they have to separate for eleven days – four days until she can begin to count[23] and then seven blood-free days.[24] During this time they have to observe all the separations incumbent upon a couple when the wife is a *niddah*.[25]

Medical Procedures

Procedures that involve opening of the cervix can lead to the onset of the *niddah* status. This is discussed in detail in Part Four, chapter 1 (pp. 144–145).

---

[23] In this case, Ashkenazim also wait 4 days rather than 5. However, if she becomes *niddah* from the onset of her menses before she goes to *mikveh* after *dam betulim*, a 5 day minimum is needed.

[24] See above.

[25] There is one difference which is discussed below in Part Three, chapter 2 (p. 124).

CHAPTER 3

THE CESSATION OF THE *NIDDAH* STATUS – COUNTING

Shiva neki'im[1]

As mentioned, any woman who has uterine bleeding today needs to follow the laws of a *zavah gedolah*, and must count seven blood-free days before going to the *mikveh*.

שִׁבְעָה יָמִים שֶׁהַזָּבָה סוֹפֶרֶת מַתְחִילִין מִמָּחֳרַת יוֹם שֶׁפַּסְקָה בּוֹ. (שולחן ערוך ; יורה דעה, קצו :א)

The seven days that a *zavah* counts were originally counted from the day following the day that she stopped bleeding. As will be explained below, today there is usually a wait of 4 or 5 days from the onset of bleeding until she begins counting.

Hefsek taharah

וְכָךְ מִשְׁפָּטָהּ, אִם תִּרְאֶה שְׁנֵי יָמִים אוֹ שְׁלֹשָׁה וּפָסְקָה מִלִּרְאוֹת, בּוֹדֶקֶת בַּיּוֹם שֶׁפַּסְקָה כְּדֵי שֶׁתִּפְסוֹק בְּטָהֳרָה. (שולחן ערוך ; יורה דעה, קצו :א)

Since a woman cannot begin counting as long as blood exits the uterus, she has to do an internal examination in order to be sure that she

---

[1] These days are often called the seven clean days, translating *naki* as clean. *Naki*, however, can also mean "free of." Therefore, we generally use "blood-free" throughout the book. This is to indicate that this is a religious state that is not related to bodily cleanliness.

has in fact stopped bleeding. This is called a *hefsek taharah* – literally, that she has stopped bleeding and thus can become *tehorah*, ritually pure.

וּמִנְהָג כָּשֵׁר הוּא: כְּשֶׁהָאִשָּׁה פּוֹסֶקֶת בְּטָהֳרָה, שֶׁתִּרְחַץ וְלוֹבֶשֶׁת לְבָנִים; אָמְנָם אִם לֹא רָחֲצָה רַק פָּנֶיהָ שֶׁל מַטָּה, דַּי בְּכָךְ, וְכֵן נוֹהֲגִין וְאֵין לְשַׁנּוֹת. (רמא; יורה דעה, קצו:ג)

Prior to doing the *hefsek taharah,* a woman should clean the external vaginal area. Ideally, she should first take a bath, as this will remove all old blood. If this is not possible, it is sufficient to wipe the external vaginal area with a wet cloth or a baby wipe. If this too is impossible, but the exam in any event shows no problematic stains, the *hefsek taharah* still counts and she can commence the *shiva neki'im*, the seven blood-free days, the following day.

The *hefsek taharah* is the most important of all internal examinations. When this type of internal examination is done at other times, it is known as a *bedikah* (*bedikot*, plural).

These internal examinations are performed as follows:

כָּל בְּדִיקוֹת אֵלּוּ – בֵּין בְּדִיקַת הֶפְסֵק טָהֳרָה, בֵּין בְּדִיקַת כָּל הַשִּׁבְעָה – צְרִיכוֹת לִהְיוֹת בְּבֶגֶד פִּשְׁתָּן לָבָן יָשָׁן אוֹ בְּצֶמֶר גֶּפֶן אוֹ בְּצֶמֶר לָבָן נָקִי וָרַךְ. וְתַכְנִיסֶנּוּ בְּאוֹתוֹ מָקוֹם בְּעוֹמֶק לַחוֹרִים וְלַסְּדָקִים עַד מָקוֹם שֶׁהַשַּׁמָּשׁ דָּשׁ, וְתִרְאֶה אִם יֵשׁ בּוֹ שׁוּם מַרְאֶה אַדְמוּמִית – וְלֹא שֶׁתַּכְנִיסֵהוּ מְעַט לְקַנֵּחַ עַצְמָהּ. (שולחן ערוך; יורה דעה, קצו:ו)

She takes a white pre-checked soft cotton cloth,[2] wraps it around her finger[3] and inserts it deeply[4] but GENTLY into the vaginal canal.[5] She then

---

[2] The sources refer to other materials that may be used, such as surgical cotton (cotton balls). However, this is not recommended, as they may contain small colored threads. Furthermore, absorbent cotton may absorb blood deeply so that it may not be visible on the surface. Anything used for a *bedikah* should be checked first for any preexisting stains, threads, etc.

[3] She also should check her finger to assure that it is clean and has no wound that could bleed onto the cloth. She should also be careful of sharp fingernails that might cause irritation or injury to the vaginal area.

[4] Ideally, this insertion should be as deep as the woman estimates that her husband's penis reaches during marital relations, although she obviously cannot go deeper than the length of her finger. If this is difficult for her, she should try to go deeply at least for the *hefsek taharah* and for one of the *bedikot* during the 7 days,

moves her finger circumferentially around the vaginal canal, GENTLY touching the sides, being careful to enter the crevices of the vaginal canal (*chorim usdakim*).[6] She then withdraws the cloth and checks it in a good light. If all discharge on the cloth is white, clear, or light yellow her bleeding is assumed to have stopped, and she can count the NEXT day as the first of her seven blood-free days. If it is obviously red, she will need to try again later.[7] If it is any other color, she should arrange to have it shown to a rabbinical authority, as other colors may in fact be acceptable.

וּבְדִיקָה זוֹ תִּהְיֶה סָמוּךְ לְבֵין הַשְּׁמָשׁוֹת. (שׁוּלחָן ערוּךְ ; יורה דעה, קצו :א)

וְכֵן נוֹהֲגִין לְכַתְּחִלָּה ; וּבְדִיעֲבַד, אֲפִילוּ לֹא בָדְקָה עַצְמָהּ רַק שַׁחֲרִית וְמָצְאָה עַצְמָהּ

טְהוֹרָה, סַגֵּי [דַּי] בְּכָךָ. (רמא ; שם)

The *hefsek taharah* must be done during the daylight hours, defined as between halachic sunrise and halachic sunset.[8] Ideally, it is done in the

---

preferably the first. However, if this is painful she should not concentrate on going deeply but rather ensure that she has gone around the vagina circumferentially (see *Shulchan Aruch* YD 196:6 and *Rema* there).

[5] Pre-prepared cloths of this type can be purchased in most *mikvaot* around the world and also in many pharmacies and supermarkets in Israel. They can be ordered over the internet via www.mikvah.org. Women can prepare these cloths themselves by cutting up well washed white cotton underwear.

[6] Learning to do a *bedikah* is quite similar to learning how to use a tampon. It helps to relax and try a number of positions, such as one foot raised on the edge of the toilet or bathtub, sitting on the toilet with legs apart, or squatting. If the *bedikah* is painful, she should consult an authority about using a lubricant such as KY Jelly. Petroleum jelly ("Vaseline"), is not recommended, as it prevents the cloth from absorbing any blood that may be present. Some authorities permit the use of petroleum jelly a few hours prior to the exam. KY Jelly, however, is water soluble, so this is less of a problem. Nevertheless, some rabbis feel that it changes the color of the stain that might be found on the *bedikah*. Wetting the cloth slightly may make the exam more comfortable. However, if the cloth is very wet, this will prevent absorption of any blood that is present.

[7] If there remains time before sunset, it is a good idea to wait a few minutes before checking a second time, to allow the natural secretions to return so the examination does not cause an abrasion.

[8] These are not always identical with the times published in newspapers. A couple should have access to a locally applicable list of such times. Such lists are generally

late afternoon[9] before sunset, but when necessary, it can be done in the morning. Busy women who have a tendency to forget (especially on short winter afternoons), and don't find these exams painful or troublesome, should do one in the morning and another in the afternoon. In this way they have a "backup" in case of forgetting. If a woman missed sunset by a few minutes she should consult a rabbi.

On *erev* Shabbat she should check before candlelighting. If the community starts Shabbat early, she should also check prior to candelighting. However, in either case, as long as she checks before sunset, the exam is valid.

Moch dachuk

לְעוֹלָם יְלַמֵּד אָדָם בְּתוֹךְ בֵּיתוֹ שֶׁתְּהֵא בוֹדֶקֶת בְּיוֹם הֶפְסֵק טָהֳרָתָהּ בְּמוֹךְ דָּחוּק וְשֶׁיְּהֵא שָׁם כָּל בֵּין הַשְּׁמָשׁוֹת, שֶׁזּוּ בְּדִיקָה מוֹצִיאָה מִידֵי כָּל סָפֵק.
(שולחן ערוך ; יורה דעה, קצו :א)

רָאֲתָה יוֹם אֶחָד בִּלְבָד וּפָסְקָה בּוֹ בַּיּוֹם, צְרִיכָה לִבְדּוֹק עַצְמָהּ בְּמוֹךְ דָּחוּק וְשֶׁיְּהֵא שָׁם כָּל בֵּין הַשְּׁמָשׁוֹת. (שלחן ערוך ; יורה דעה, קצו :ב)
הרמא מוסיף :
לְהַחְמִיר לְכַתְּחִלָּה [לעשות מוך דחוק]
וּבְדִיעֲבַד, אִם בָּדְקָה עַצְמָהּ סָמוּךְ לְבֵין הַשְּׁמָשׁוֹת וּמָצְאָה עַצְמָהּ טְהוֹרָה –אַף עַל פִּי שֶׁלֹּא הָיְתָה אֶצְלָהּ הַמּוֹךְ כָּל בֵּין הַשְּׁמָשׁוֹת – סַגִּי ; אֲבָל בְּדִיקַת שַׁחֲרִית לֹא מְהַנֵּי [מוֹעִיל], הוֹאִיל וְלֹא רָאֲתָה רַק יוֹם אֶחָד. (רמא ; שם)

While the purpose of the *hefsek taharah* is to demonstrate that all bleeding has ceased, there is still room for doubt that perhaps some bleeding from the uterus into the vagina occurred afterwards. Therefore, the custom of a *moch dachuk* – literally, closely packed wadding – has evolved. This involves filling the vaginal canal with a cloth starting from sunset and ending after nightfall. In Israel, this is generally about 20 minutes; in some communities

---

available through local synagogues or can be found on the internet via the Nishmat Women's Health and Halacha webste www.yoatzot.org.

[9] It is best NOT to wait until the last possible moment prior to sunset. Doing so does not leave time for a repeat if the first attempt is not valid and it is likely to lead to possible completion AFTER sunset. Rushing can also lead to abrasions.

outside Israel, it is longer. A local halachic authority may be consulted. This is generally done by taking a *bedikah* cloth[10] and inserting it into the vaginal canal. Some authorities permit the use of a tampon for this purpose. It is a good idea to sit or lie down during this period, to prevent irritation of the vaginal wall that can cause stains from vaginal rather than uterine blood. Women who find this exam uncomfortable should consult an authority. Similarly, during times when her vaginal lining is sensitive, such as after childbirth, she should consult a rabbi to determine whether the *moch* is necessary. If she performed a *hefsek taharah* but forgot the *moch*, the *hefsek taharah* is still valid and she can count the next day as the first of the *shiva neki'im*.[11]

Wearing white

בְּיוֹם שֶׁפָּסְקָה מִלִּרְאוֹת וּבוֹדֶקֶת עַצְמָהּ כָּאָמוּר, תִּלְבַּשׁ חָלוּק הַבָּדוּק לָהּ שֶׁאֵין בּוֹ כֶּתֶם, וּבַלַּיְלָה תָּשִׂים סְדִינִים הַבְּדוּקִים מִכְּתָמִים, וּמִיּוֹם הַמָּחֳרָת תַּתְחִיל לִסְפּוֹר שִׁבְעָה נְקִיִּים. (שלחן ערוך ; יורה דעה, קצו :ג)

אֲבָל בִּשְׁעַת הַדְּחָק, כְּגוֹן אִשָּׁה הַהוֹלֶכֶת בַּדֶּרֶךְ וְאֵין לָהּ בְּגָדִים, תּוּכַל לִסְפּוֹר שִׁבְעָה נְקִיִּים – רַק שֶׁהֶחָלוּק יִהְיֶה נָקִי וּבָדוּק מֵהֶם. (רמא ; שם)

After a woman does the *hefsek taharah*, she needs to determine that for the next seven days she has no more bleeding. For this purpose, women wore clothes that were pre-checked to be stain-free and used stain-free sheets so that any new stain would be immediately apparent. Later, the custom evolved to use white linens and hence these seven blood-free days are also known as יְמֵי לִיבוּנָה or her "white days." Now that women wear form-fitting underpants, many authorities rule that white underwear is sufficient without the need for white clothes or white sheets, as long as she

---

[10] If one cloth is too loose for her, she can use two *bedikah* cloths.

[11] However, if her bleeding started earlier on that same day (and not on a previous day), she has a status of *"maayan patuach"* (an open fountain) which makes a *moch dachuk* mandatory. Some authorities are similarly concerned about any day on which she earlier saw blood.

sleeps with undergarments.[12] The custom of using white underwear during these days has become widely accepted. However, if she has none available, she does not need to postpone counting the seven blood-free days, but she should wear other pre-checked clean colored underwear until white is available.[13]

Bedikot (internal exams)

בְּכָל יוֹם מִשִּׁבְעָה יְמֵי הַסְּפִירָה, צְרִיכָה לִהְיוֹת בּוֹדֶקֶת לְכַתְּחִלָּה פַּעֲמַיִם בְּכָל יוֹם –
אַחַת שַׁחֲרִית וְאַחַת סָמוּךְ לְבֵין הַשְּׁמָשׁוֹת. (שלחן ערוך ; יורה דעה, קצו:ד)

On each of the seven days (which she begins to count from the day AFTER the *hefsek*), she needs to be certain that she remains blood-free. This is done by internal examinations as described for the *hefsek taharah*. Ideally, she should do two exams per day, one in the morning after sunrise[14] and one in the afternoon before sunset.[15] However, if the exams are painful, uncomfortable, or cause her to feel that she is irritating herself, she should consult a rabbi as to how to reduce the number. If on any day she missed one of the two exams for any reason, e.g., forgetting, being in a place where she could not do the exam, she should continue to check the next day as usual. If she missed *both* examinations on one day in the middle of her *shiva neki'im* (days 2-6), she should continue to check the next day as usual. However, if she missed both examinations on *day one* or *day seven*, she will need to delay her immersion and should consult a rabbi as to how to proceed. Fortunately, these days are relatively easy to remember: day one is

---

[12] Some people still keep the custom of white sheets. Others are embarrassed by other people being able to infer from their white sheets that the wife is currently *niddah* and will soon go to the *mikveh*.

[13] This need for white underwear applies only during the seven blood-free days. Once they are completed, even if she has not yet gone to the *mikveh* she can change to colored. Thus, she can change into colored underwear prior to going to the *mikveh* late that night, or if she can't get to the *mikveh* until the following evening; for example, when her *mikveh* night is Friday night and there is no *mikveh* within walking distance.

[14] She can do this whenever she awakes. She does not have to wake up at sunrise.

[15] A *bedikah* done after sundown cannot count towards the day that ended at sunset. However, it can count, if needed, towards a *bedikah* of the next day.

the day after the *hefsek taharah*, and she will immerse in the mikveh the night after completing day seven.

Minimum days prior to starting *shiva neki'im*

The reason for the waiting period before the start of the seven blood-free days, is as follows:

הַפּוֹלֶטֶת שִׁכְבַת זֶרַע בִּימֵי סְפִירָתָהּ – אִם הוּא תּוֹךְ שֵׁשׁ עוֹנוֹת לְשִׁמּוּשָׁהּ, סוֹתֶרֶת אוֹתוֹ יוֹם. לְפִיכָךְ, הַמְשַׁמֶּשֶׁת מִטָּתָהּ וְרָאֲתָה אַחַר כָּךְ וּפָסְקָה, אֵינָהּ מַתְחֶלֶת לִסְפּוֹר שִׁבְעָה נְקִיִּים עַד שֶׁיַּעַבְרוּ עָלֶיהָ שֵׁשׁ עוֹנוֹת שְׁלֵמוֹת שֶׁמָּא תִפְלוֹט; לְפִיכָךְ, אֵינָהּ מַתְחֶלֶת לִסְפּוֹר עַד יוֹם הַחֲמִישִׁי לְשִׁמּוּשָׁהּ: כְּגוֹן, אִם שִׁמְּשָׁה בְּמוֹצָאֵי שַׁבָּת, אֵינָהּ מַתְחֶלֶת לִסְפּוֹר עַד יוֹם חֲמִישִׁי, דְּקַיְמָא לָן אֵין שִׁכְבַת זֶרַע מַסְרִיחַ עַד שֶׁיַּעַבְרוּ עָלָיו שֵׁשׁ עוֹנוֹת שְׁלֵמוֹת מֵעֵת לְעֵת. וְאִם שִׁמְּשָׁה בְּמוֹצָאֵי שַׁבָּת, וּפָלְטָה לֵיל רְבִיעִי קוֹדֶם עֵת שִׁימוּשָׁהּ בְּמוֹצָאֵי שַׁבָּת – עֲדַיִן הִיא עוֹמֶדֶת בְּתוֹךְ עוֹנָה שְׁשִׁית לְשִׁמּוּשָׁהּ וְסוֹתֶרֶת, הִילְכָּךְ יוֹם חֲמִישִׁי יִהְיֶה רִאשׁוֹן לִסְפִירָתָהּ. (שלחן ערוך ; יורה דעה, קצו:יא)

As explained in the *Shulchan Aruch*, the day on which a woman expels viable semen from her body cannot be counted as one of the seven blood-free days. Halachically, semen is considered viable for 72 hours.[16] After that point even if it is expelled, it is of no halachic consequence.

A woman might not be aware that she is expelling semen, and thus invalidate one of her seven blood-free days without realizing it. (This could happen if she had intercourse just before the onset of *niddah*, had only one or two days of bleeding, and immediately performed a *hefsek taharah*.) Therefore, she needs to wait for 72 hours from the time she had intercourse until she begins to count.[17]

The *Rema*, however, outlines the Ashkenazi custom:

וְיֵשׁ שֶׁכָּתְבוּ שֶׁיֵּשׁ לְהַמְתִּין עוֹד יוֹם אֶחָד, דְּהַיְנוּ, שֶׁלֹּא תַּתְחִיל לִמְנוֹת עַד יוֹם הַשִּׁשִּׁי וְהוּא יִהְיֶה יוֹם רִאשׁוֹן לִסְפִירָתָהּ, דְּחָיְישִׁינַן שֶׁמָּא עַל תְּשַׁמֵּשׁ בַּיּוֹם הָרִאשׁוֹן בֵּין הַשְּׁמָשׁוֹת וְתִסְבּוֹר שֶׁהוּא יוֹם, וְאֶפְשָׁר שֶׁהוּא לַיְלָה, וְאִם תַּתְחִיל לִמְנוֹת מִיּוֹם חֲמִישִׁי, יִהְיֶה תּוֹךְ שֵׁשׁ עוֹנוֹת לְשִׁמּוּשָׁהּ. עַל כֵּן יֵשׁ לְהוֹסִיף עוֹד יוֹם אֶחָד, דְּמֵעַתָּה אִי אֶפְשָׁר לָבֹא לִידֵי טָעוּת; וְכֵן נוֹהֲגִין בְּכָל מְדִינוֹת אֵלּוּ, וְאֵין לְשַׁנּוֹת. (רמא ; יורה דעה, קצו:יא)

---

[16] This is also the medically-established length of time that sperm are viable in the uterus.

[17] גזרו אינה פולטת אטו פולטת.

A woman who has intercourse between sunset and full darkness might mistakenly begin her count one day too early. Therefore, there is a further safeguard to add an extra day, and to begin counting the seven blood-free days no earlier than the sixth day from the onset of *niddah*. This procedure is followed by all Ashkenazi communities but not by all Sephardi communities.

The need for a five day minimum prior to starting the *shiva neki'im* has been extended even to situations where she did not have intercourse immediately prior to the onset of her menses.[18] If she saw blood immediately after a day when intercourse was in any case halachically forbidden,[19] such as Yom Kippur or Tishah B'Av, it can be counted as the first of the five (or four) days.[20]

In pressing circumstances, such as difficulty in conceiving, or travel by one member of the couple, there is room for leniency even for Ashkenazi women to wait only four days before the *hefsek taharah*. Thus, if a woman has extenuating circumstances, and her menses do not last five days, she should consult a rabbi.

Examples of counting

To summarize, we will give a few examples:

Tevet

Sat	Fri	Thur	Wed	Tues	Mon	Sun
ב	א					
ט	# ח	# ז	# ו	# ה	# ד	ג
טז	טו	יד	יג	יב	יא	י
כג	כב	כא	כ	יט	יח	יז
	כט	כח	כז	כו	כה	כד

---

18 גזרו לא שמשה אטו שמשה.

19 But generally not because of merely medical reasons or that her husband was not around. Nevertheless, when necessary, one should always ask the question.

20 *Igrot Moshe*, YD 4:17(21)

She bled on each day marked with a #. She started on Monday, the 4th of *Tevet*, at 10:00 am (during the daytime *onah*). She did a *hefsek taharah* on Friday, the 8th of *Tevet* (day number five of bleeding) in the afternoon, and it was acceptable. She then placed a *moch dachuk* right before sunset and left it in place for 20 minutes. The next morning, Shabbat the 9th of *Tevet*, was the first day of the seven clean days, and Friday, the 15th of *Tevet*, was the seventh. Assuming all the *bedikot* were acceptable, she immersed in the *mikveh* on Friday night.

Shvat

Sat	Fri	Thur	Wed	Tues	Mon	Sun
א						
ח	# ז	# ו	# ה	ד	ג	ב
טו	יד	יג	יב	יא	י	ט
כב	כא	כ	יט	יח	יז	טז
כט	כח	כז	כו	כה	כד	כג
						ל

Here she bled for three days, starting Tuesday night at 10 pm. As the Hebrew day begins at sunset, this was already considered Wednesday and she thus bled on the 5th, 6th and 7th of *Shvat*. Assuming she is Ashkenazic and has no extenuating circumstances, she cannot count the first of the seven blood-free days until the 10th of *Shvat*, as five days need to have passed. Normally she would do the *hefsek taharah* on Sunday, the 9th of *Shvat*, in the afternoon, although if at that time she would not have water available for washing or if there were other problems,[21] she could do it as early as Friday the 7th after the bleeding stopped.[22] In either case, the first of the *shiva neki'im* was Monday, the 10th of *Shvat*, and the last was Sunday,

---

[21] Such as being on a camping trip with little access to water or privacy.

[22] Doing the *hefsek* early has the added advantage of ending early the stringencies of the first three days. One has to be careful, however, to start the seven blood-free days only at the appropriate time (after 5 days have passed).

the 16th of *Shvat*. If all *bedikot* were acceptable, she immersed in the *mikveh* Sunday night.

Adar

Sat	Fri	Thur	Wed	Tues	Mon	Sun
# ו	# ה	# ד	# ג	ב	א	
יג	יב	יא	י	# ט	ח	# ז
כ	יט	יח	יז	טז	טו	יד
כז	כו	כה	כד	כג	כב	כא
					כט	כח

She started bleeding on Wednesday morning, the 3rd of *Adar*. She bled for five days and obtained a clean *hefsek taharah* on Sunday afternoon, the 7th of *Adar*. She placed a *moch dachuk*, which was fine, as were the *bedikot* on the first "clean" day, Monday, the 8th. On Tuesday, the 9th of *Adar*, however, the morning *bedikah* was somewhat painful and she had a red stain on the *bedikah* cloth. In this case, she had to begin the seven clean days over. As she had already waited five days and had remained halachically forbidden to have relations, she did not need to wait the initial five days again. She did a *hefsek taharah* later on that same Tuesday in the afternoon, which was acceptable. She asked a rabbi if she needed to do a *moch dachuk* this time, and he told her that since there had been only one new day of bleeding, a *moch* was necessary,[23] but due to her feeling that perhaps she had some local irritation, she subsequently need do only one *bedikah* per day. The *moch dachuk* was acceptable, as were the daily exams from Wednesday the 10th of *Adar* through Tuesday the 16th of *Adar*. She went to the *mikveh* Tuesday night.

---

[23] As discussed above, the rules of *moch dachuk* are more stringent if there is bleeding for only one day (*Shulchan Aruch* and *Rema* YD 196:2)

CHAPTER 4

THE CESSATION OF THE *NIDDAH* STATUS – *MIKVEH*

Need for *mikveh* immersion

Finishing menses and counting seven clean days are necessary for the cessation of the *niddah* status, but not sufficient.

אֵין הַנִּדָּה וְהַזָּבָה וְהַיּוֹלֶדֶת עוֹלוֹת מִטּוּמְאָתָן בְּלֹא טְבִילָה, שֶׁאֲפִילוּ אַחַר כַּמָּה שָׁנִים חַיָּיב כָּרֵת הַבָּא עַל אַחַת מֵהֶן, אֶלָּא אִם כֵּן טָבְלוּ כָּרָאוּי בְּמִקְוֶה הָרָאוּי.
(שולחן ערוך ; יורה דעה, קצז:א)

Even if years have gone by since her last menses, a woman retains the status of *niddah* with all its attendant prohibitions until she immerses properly in a proper *mikveh*.

When does one immerse in the *mikveh*

אֲסוּרָה לִטְבּוֹל בַּיּוֹם הַשְּׁבִיעִי ; וַאֲפִילוּ אִם מַמְתֶּנֶת מִלִּטְבּוֹל עַד יוֹם הַשְּׁמִינִי אוֹ תְּשִׁיעִי, אֵינָהּ יְכוֹלָה לִטְבּוֹל בַּיּוֹם מִשּׁוּם סֶרֶךְ בִּתָּהּ. (שולחן ערוך ; יורה דעה, קצז:ג)

As mentioned above (p. 24), by biblical law a *niddah* could immerse on the night following the completion of seven days from the onset of bleeding (i.e., the beginning of the eighth day). A *zavah* could immerse during the daylight hours of the seventh day of the blood free-days, although she could not resume marital relations until nightfall. However, the rabbis decreed that the *zavah* must also wait for nightfall before immersing, so as not to lead to temptation. Thus, today a woman must postpone her *mikveh* immersion until after nightfall – when the stars come out – about the same time that Shabbat is over that week.[1] The rabbis further decreed that even if for some reason she immersed on a later date than needed, she should still wait until nightfall. The reason is מִשׁוּם סֶרֶךְ בִּתָּה ("because of the conduct of her daughter") meaning that her daughter might see her[2] immerse during daylight on the eighth (or later) day and mistakenly conclude that daytime immersion is permissible on the seventh day as well.

הֵיכָא דְּאִיכָּא אוֹנֶס – כְּגוֹן שֶׁיְּרֵאָה לִטְבּוֹל בַּלַּיְלָה מֵחֲמַת צִינָה אוֹ פַּחַד גַּנָּבִים וְכַיּוֹצֵא בּוֹ, אוֹ שֶׁסוֹגְרִין שַׁעֲרֵי הָעִיר – יְכוֹלָה לִטְבּוֹל בַּשְּׁמִינִי מִבְּעוֹד יוֹם ; אֲבָל בַּשְּׁבִיעִי לֹא תִּטְבּוֹל מִבְּעוֹד יוֹם, אַף עַל גַּב דְּאִיכָּא אוֹנֶס. (שולחן ערוך ; יורה דעה, קצז:ד)

In pressing circumstances (e.g., the *mikveh* being located in an area that is unsafe at night), it may be permitted to immerse during the daylight hours of the EIGHTH day, but a rabbi should be consulted for this determination. A bride prior to her wedding may immerse during daylight hours.

Preparation for *mikveh* – why

צְרִיכָה שֶׁתִּטְבּוֹל כָּל גּוּפָהּ בְּפַעַם אַחַת; לְפִיכָךְ, צָרִיךְ שֶׁלֹּא יִהְיֶה עָלֶיהָ שׁוּם דָּבָר הַחוֹצֵץ. (שולחן ערוך ; יורה דעה, קצח:א)

---

[1] If she does not have access to a calendar with the exact time for that evening, she should estimate the time Shabbat was out the PREVIOUS week during that part of the year that the days are getting longer, or the FOLLOWING week at the time that the days are getting shorter.

[2] While it may sound strange to us that her daughter knows when she is going to the *mikveh*, in the days when ritual purity for foods was practiced, everyone used to be aware of a woman's *niddah* status. In fact, women then wore special clothes when they were menstruating. Today, Ashkenazim are particular about not revealing when a woman goes to the *mikveh*, based on the *Rema* at the end of YD 198:

יֵשׁ שֶׁכָּתְבוּ שֶׁיֵּשׁ לְאִשָּׁה לִהְיוֹת צְנוּעָה בְּלֵיל טְבִילָתָהּ; וְכֵן נָהֲגוּ הַנָּשִׁים לְהַסְתִּיר לֵיל טְבִילָתָן שֶׁלֹּא יֵלֵךְ בִּמְהוּמָה אוֹ בִּפְנֵי הַבְּרִיּוֹת שֶׁלֹּא יַרְגִּישׁוּ בָּהֶן בְּנֵי אָדָם.

Many Sephardim, however, are not particular about this.

For immersion in the *mikveh*, the entire body has to be submerged under the water at the same time. This is derived from the juxtaposition of verses speaking of immersing in the *mikveh* and of the setting of the sun.

נֶפֶשׁ אֲשֶׁר תִּגַּע בּוֹ וְטָמְאָה עַד הָעֶרֶב וְלֹא יֹאכַל מִן הַקֳּדָשִׁים כִּי אִם רָחַץ בְּשָׂרוֹ בַּמָּיִם. וּבָא הַשֶּׁמֶשׁ וְטָהֵר וְאַחַר יֹאכַל מִן הַקֳּדָשִׁים כִּי לַחְמוֹ הוּא. (ויקרא כב:ו–ז)

Just as the sun sets completely, so the entire body needs to be immersed completely. Thus, if there is any barrier between the body and the water, one cannot just re-immerse the part of the body on which the barrier had been, but one must re-immerse the entire body. Such a barrier is known as a *chatzitzah*.

דַּאֲמַר רַבִּי יִצְחָק: דְּבַר תּוֹרָה, רֻבּוֹ וּמַקְפִּיד עָלָיו – חוֹצֵץ, וְשֶׁאֵינוֹ מַקְפִּיד עָלָיו – אֵינוֹ חוֹצֵץ. וְגָזְרוּ עַל רֻבּוֹ שֶׁאֵינוֹ מַקְפִּיד מִשּׁוּם רֻבּוֹ הַמַּקְפִּיד, וְעַל מִעוּטוֹ הַמַּקְפִּיד מִשּׁוּם רֻבּוֹ הַמַּקְפִּיד. וְלִיגְזוֹר נַמִי עַל מִעוּטוֹ שֶׁאֵינוֹ מַקְפִּיד מִשּׁוּם מִעוּטוֹ הַמַּקְפִּיד, אִי נַמִי מִשּׁוּם רֻבּוֹ שֶׁאֵינוֹ מַקְפִּיד! הִיא גוּפָה גְּזֵירָה, וְאֲנַן נֵיקוּם וְנִיגְזוֹר גְּזֵירָה לִגְזֵירָה? (תלמוד בבלי, עירובין ד:)

Under biblical law, in order to be considered a *chatzitzah* and invalidate the immersion, the barrier would have to cover most of the body (*rov*), and the person would have to mind the presence of this substance (*makpid*). In order to safeguard this important commandment, however, the rabbis decreed that even a barrier covering most of the body which she does not mind, or one which she does mind even if it covers only a small part of the body, is considered a barrier that invalidates immersion.

וַאֲפִילוּ כָּל שֶׁהוּא – אִם דֶּרֶךְ בְּנֵי אָדָם לְפְעָמִים לְהַקְפִּיד עָלָיו – חוֹצֵץ. אֲפִילוּ אִם אֵינָהּ מַקְפֶּדֶת עָלָיו עַתָּה, אוֹ אֲפִילוּ אֵינָהּ מַקְפֶּדֶת עָלָיו לְעוֹלָם – כֵּיוָן שֶׁדֶּרֶךְ רוֹב בְּנֵי אָדָם לְהַקְפִּיד עָלָיו – חוֹצֵץ. וְאִם הוּא חוֹפֶה רוֹב הַגּוּף, אֲפִילוּ אֵין דֶּרֶךְ בְּנֵי אָדָם לְהַקְפִּיד בְּכָךְ – חוֹצֵץ. (שולחן ערוך; יורה דעה, קצח:א)

וּלְכַתְּחִלָּה לֹא תִּטְבּוֹל אֲפִילוּ בִּדְבָרִים שֶׁאֵינָם חוֹצְצִין, גְּזֵרָה אַטוּ דְּבָרִים הַחוֹצְצִים. (רמא; שם)

The halacha at present is that a barrier of any size is significant if it is of a kind that most people would mind having there, even if the woman who is about to immerse does not mind its presence (now or ever). Therefore, every attempt is made to remove even small amounts of foreign material. If there are special circumstances, other principles come into play in determining whether the item is, in fact, a barrier. Some examples are:

1. She wants the item there for cosmetic purposes (e.g., hair color).

2. Removal would be dangerous.

3. The item performs a medical role (e.g., stitches).

4. It is permanently attached to her body.

Therefore, a rabbinical authority should be consulted about such items and one should assume neither that they are <u>not</u> a problem, nor that they <u>are</u> a problem and thus delay immersing in the *mikveh*.

Preparation for *mikveh* – how

לְעוֹלָם יְלַמֵּד אָדָם בְּתוֹךְ בֵּיתוֹ שֶׁתְּהֵא אִשָּׁה מְדִיחָה קְמָטֶיהָ וְכָל בֵּית סְתָרֶיהָ בְּמַיִם וְשֶׁתְּהֵא חוֹפֶפֶת שְׂעַר רֹאשָׁהּ וְשֶׁתְּהֵא סוֹרֶקֶת יָפֶה בְּמַסְרֵק שֶׁלֹּא יִהְיוּ נִדְבָּקִין זֶה בְּזֶה, שֶׁזּוֹ הִיא מְתַקֶּנֶת עֶזְרָא שֶׁתְּהֵא אִשָּׁה חוֹפֶפֶת בִּשְׁעַת טְבִילָה... וְנָהֲגוּ בְּנוֹת יִשְׂרָאֵל לִרְחוֹץ וְלָחוּף כָּל גּוּפָן בְּמַיִם וּמִנְהָג כָּשֵׁר הוּא... דִּין תּוֹרָה שֶׁתְּהֵא הַטּוֹבֶלֶת מְעַיֶּנֶת בְּעַצְמָהּ סָמוּךְ לִטְבִילָה וּבוֹדֶקֶת כָּל גּוּפָהּ שֶׁמָּא יֵשׁ בָּהּ דָּבָר שֶׁחוֹצֵץ בִּטְבִילָה. וְעֶזְרָא וּבֵית דִּינוֹ תִּקְנוּ שֶׁתְּהֵא חוֹפֶפֶת בְּכָל מְקוֹם שֵׂעָר שֶׁבָּהּ בְּמַיִם חַמִּין וְסוֹרֶקֶת אוֹתָן אוֹ מְפַסְפֶּסֶת אוֹתָן בְּיָדֶיהָ יָפֶה יָפֶה כְּדֵי שֶׁתַּתִּיר שַׂעֲרוֹתֶיהָ אִם יֵשׁ בָּהֶם קֶשֶׁר.

(טור ; יורה דעה, קצט)

Ensuring that there are no barriers is a two-part process. Part one is cleansing to remove any possible barrier, and part two is checking to insure that all barriers have in fact been removed.

Cleansing

The cleansing consists of a number of steps:

1. Removing obvious foreign material, e.g., clothing, rings, necklaces, earrings and other jewelry, contact lenses, which themselves are barriers.[3]

2. Washing hair with warm water.[4] This is known as *chafifah*, and is one of ten enactments (*takanot*) of Ezra.[5] Hair that is naturally attached is not a *chatzitzah*.[6] Therefore, one is not required to shave, cut, or wax one's hair as part of preparation for *mikveh*.[7] However, since there is an opinion that something about to be removed is considered a *chatzitzah*, if a woman is about to cut her hair it should be done before immersion rather than after.

Knots in the hair are a form of *chatzitzah* and must be removed. Hair on the head is thoroughly combed with a comb, while for other hair such as in the genital or underarm areas, separating the strands with fingers is sufficient.[8]

3. Washing the entire body with water.[9] Preferably, this is done with warm water (as there is a minority opinion that the *takanah* of Ezra applies to the entire body and not just to hair). However, if there is a shortage of warm water, the

---

[3] Even if water can permeate the item, if she is concerned that it might be ruined or lost it is still a *chatzitzah*, according to most opinions.

[4] Shampoo can be used to assure the hair is clean, but some conditioners may be problematic if they leave a film on the hair.

[5] *Baba Kama* 82a

[6] This includes leg and underarm hair as well.

[7] If hair is shaved, cut or waxed before going to the *mikveh*, it is important to allow time to remove the cut hairs or wax, which <u>are</u> a barrier.

[8] *Badei Hashulchan* 199:11

[9] As this washing is for a purpose and not for pleasure, it is permitted during the nine-day morning period that precedes the ninth of *Av*.

body can be washed in cold water and the warm water saved for washing the hair. While the general custom is to bathe, a shower is acceptable as long as one is careful to wash the entire body.

4. Certain parts of the body require special attention. This includes the armpits, under the breasts and other crevices known as *beit hastarim* – hidden places. Some internal parts such as the mouth are also included in this category. While the water does not have to actually reach these areas, they need to be clean enough that water could reach them.[10] Therefore, teeth must be cleaned, well-brushed and flossed.[11]

5. Using the bathroom before immersion is recommended. Nevertheless, if she forgot to do so, this does not invalidate the immersion.

6. The custom is to cut nails short, as dirt beneath nails is a form of *chatzitzah*. However, nails themselves are not a *chatzitzah*, and thus if she has a professional or emotional need for her nails to be long this is OK, as long as they are well-cleaned.[12]

7. Makeup should be removed. If she has permanent makeup, hair dye or a well-maintained manicure that she is reluctant to remove, she should consult an authority.

---

[10] רָאוּי לְבִיאַת מָיִם.

[11] *"Kmatim"* are the folds of the body. *Beit hastarim* are places that open directly to the outside, such as the mouth. There is some disagreement among the commentators about what fits into each category.

[12] Some *mikvaot* are quite particular about this custom. If a woman plans to leave her nails clean but long she should discuss this in advance with the *mikveh* attendant to prevent any unpleasantness.

8. Bandages should be removed. In the case of items that cannot be removed for medical reasons, she should consult a rabbi.

Inspection

Checking one's body for barriers is known as *iyun* and is considered a biblical commandment.[13] All parts of the body that she can see should be visually inspected. All other parts should be felt to assure that there is no foreign material. *Chafifah* is also a form of inspection. For a practical checklist for *mikveh* preparation, see Appendix E (pp.209–211).

While it is not a halachic requirement,[14] the time when a woman is preparing for the *mikveh* is a perfect time to do a breast self-exam.[15] *Mikveh* use is generally at a consistent time of the menstrual cycle,[16] she is undressed and inspecting her body anyway and a mirror is usually available.[17] This is also an ideal time to do self-screening for skin cancer.[18]

---

[13] *Tur* YD 189

[14] Nevertheless, it is certainly in fulfillment of the commandment to care for one's health.

[15] This is my personal feeling and a position endorsed by organizations such as Hadassah Women who have placed instructions for breast self-exam in many *mikvaot*. Others argue that this will make women nervous and if they find a lump it will ruin their evening with their husband. If women feel that this would make them nervous, it is possible to do it at another time – day one of one's period is the time that is generally recommended. However, in my experience, it is a rare occasion for a woman to have the uninterrupted time to focus on her body the way she can while preparing for the *mikveh*. That is why I still feel that this practice of doing it at the *mikveh* should be encouraged.

[16] As the breasts undergo changes during the month in response to changing hormones, it is recommended that a breast self-exam be done at the same time each month. Generally, the professional literature suggests the first day of the menstrual cycle, as this is an easy day to remember. However, for *mikveh* using women, midcycle is easy to remember and often more convenient.

[17] A breast self-exam is done in two steps. The first is to stand in front of a mirror with hands on the hips and observe the breasts for any change. The next is to palpate the breasts in a circular motion from the chest wall out to the nipple, feeling for any lumps. If she feels anything on one side that she does not feel on the other she should consult her physician. Usually these lumps are benign, but they should be checked to assure that in fact they are.

Preparation for *mikveh* – when

Iyun needs to be done just prior to immersing. Concerning the timing of *chafifah*, there is a disagreement that appears first in the Talmud.[19] According to one opinion, it is best to do it at night, directly before immersing in the *mikveh*. According to the other, it is best to do it earlier during the day, since if a woman waits until nighttime, she may be in a rush to get finished and not prepare properly. The custom (under ideal circumstances) is to follow both opinions by starting during the day and continuing into the night. However, if circumstances (work, young children, availability of water) preclude one option, the other is acceptable.

There are times when for halachic reasons one option is precluded. Since washing hair is not permitted on Shabbat or *Yom Tov*, if a woman plans to go to the *mikveh* Friday night, she has to prepare during the day. If she plans to go to the *mikveh* Saturday night, on the other hand, she cannot wash her hair Shabbat morning, and Friday is too far before the time of immersion. Here it appears that the proper time would be Saturday night. However, it is best to do some preparation on Friday[20] and repeat it on Saturday night. In all circumstances, inspection must be done just prior to immersing.

Preparation for *mikveh* – where

Preparation for the *mikveh* can be done at home or at the *mikveh*, whichever is more convenient. Most modern *mikvaot* have preparation rooms with showers and/or bathtubs. In America, they generally are supplied with all the equipment one would need (soap, shampoo, towels, etc). In Israel, a

---

A clinical breast exam by a health professional is recommended yearly for all women. Women over age 40 should discuss with their physician when, in light of personal or family history, a mammogram is recommended.

[18] While looking at her skin for potential barriers, she should note any new or unusual "moles" or growths, particularly if they have irregular borders. If she finds any, she should show them to her physician or consult a dermatologist.

[19] *Niddah* 66b–67a

[20] Bathing and hairwashing on Friday for Shabbat can count as this partial pre-*mikveh* preparation as well.

woman is expected to bring the supplies she needs from home, but they are often available for rent/purchase if needed.[21]

וְכֵן מִנְהָג כָּשֵׁר שֶׁאַף עַל פִּי שֶׁחָפְפָה, תִּשָּׂא עִמָּה מַסְרֵק לְבֵית הַטְּבִילָה וְתִסְרוֹק שָׁם.
(שולחן ערוך ; יורה דעה, קצט:ג)

If she prepared at home, she should comb through her hair again at the *mikveh*, and wet her body and hair with a quick shower.[22] This is to help assure that her hair will not float on top of the water and that all parts of her body will be in contact with the *mikveh* waters.

Immersing in the *mikveh* – when

אִם בַּעֲלָהּ בָּעִיר, מִצְוָה לִטְבּוֹל בִּזְמַנָּהּ שֶׁלֹּא לְבַטֵּל מִפְּרִיָּה וְרִבְיָה אֲפִילוּ לַיְלָה אַחַת.
(שולחן ערוך ; יורה דעה, קצז:ב)

If both husband and wife are in town, it is best to go to the *mikveh* on the first permissible night so as not to delay the *mitzvot* of onah (marital relations) and *pru urevu* (procreation).

וּמוּתֶּרֶת לִטְבּוֹל לֵיל שַׁבָּת... וְדַוְקָא אִם בַּעֲלָהּ בָּעִיר, אֲבָל בְּלָאו הָכִי [וְאִם] לֹא כָּךְ אָסוּר. (רמא ; שם)

This halachic preference to immerse on time overrides concerns about using the *mikveh* on Shabbat.[23] Therefore, one does immerse on Friday night, if the couple is together.[24] If either member of the couple is out of town, the wife does not immerse on Shabbat (Friday night) or *Yom Tov*. If one member of the couple is away on a weekday night, there are differenc-

---

[21] There is generally a fee for the use of the *mikveh*, to aid in its upkeep. On Shabbat and holidays no payment is asked for, but one should pay at a later time.

[22] This is the meaning of the common question asked on arriving at the *mikveh*: Do you want a shower (i.e., Did you prepare at home) or a bath (i.e., Do you plan to prepare here)?

[23] See discussion below.

[24] Even if she could have immersed on an earlier night, today the custom is to immerse Friday night when the couple is together.

es of opinion whether it is preferable to immerse on schedule[25] or to wait for the spouse to return.[26]

Special considerations for Friday night or *Yom Tov*

Many elements of preparations for immersion are prohibited or restricted on Shabbat and *Yom Tov*. Therefore, a woman who plans to immerse in the *mikveh* on Friday night or the night of *Yom Tov* should complete her preparations at home before she lights candles. This includes bathing, washing and combing hair, and cutting nails.

Since she prepared at home, she needs to re-wet her body at the *mikveh*. During the week, she would do this by taking a quick shower. However, bathing on Shabbat is normally forbidden, particularly in warm water. Furthermore, using most baths and showers will automatically lead to heating of more hot water, which is forbidden on Shabbat. Therefore, rather than taking a cold shower, many women immerse once in the *mikveh* waters (which are heated prior to Shabbat) to wet themselves before the halachically significant immersion. Some *mikvaot*, however, are equipped with showers designed for use on Shabbat. One should clarify the proper procedure with the *mikveh* attendant before entering the preparation room. An additional consideration when using the *mikveh* on Shabbat is that one needs to be careful not to squeeze water out of one's hair or towel.

On Shabbat and *Yom Tov*, just as on any other day, a woman needs to visually inspect herself for before immersing. If she finds a problem, she should ask the *mikveh* attendant how to proceed. Due to the laws of Shabbat and *Yom Tov*, the procedures may be different than on a weekday.

Immersing in the *mikveh* – how

Immersing in the *mikveh* generally involves walking down stairs into the water.[27]

---

[25] See *Bnei Banim* Vol 2 number 33.

[26] This opinion is mentioned by a number of latter-day *poskim*. It is based on kabbalistic sources.

[27] For a woman who has difficulty walking, *mikvaot* are available with lifts, or she can be carried by other women.

אָמַר רֵישׁ לָקִישׁ: הָאִשָּׁה לֹא תִּטְבּוֹל אֶלָּא דֶרֶךְ גְּדִילָתָהּ. כִּדְתְנַן: ...אִשָּׁה נִרְאֵית
כְּאוֹרֶגֶת וּכְמֵנִיקָה אֶת בְּנָהּ. (תלמוד בבלי, נדה סז.)

The ideal position for immersion is "as if she is weaving or nursing her child" – slightly crouched, hands extended, fingers slightly apart, eyes and mouth closed gently, in such a way that all of her body and her hair are under the water. However, if it is difficult for her to assume this position, she should wet all parts of her body with the water of the *mikveh* and immerse in any way that her whole body is submerged.[28]

צָרִיךְ לַעֲמוֹד עַל גַּבָּהּ יְהוּדִית גְּדוֹלָה יוֹתֵר מִשְׁתֵּים עֶשְׂרֵה שָׁנָה וְיוֹם אֶחָד בְּשָׁעָה שֶׁהִיא
טוֹבֶלֶת, שֶׁתִּרְאֶה שֶׁלֹּא יִשָּׁאֵר מִשְׂעַר רֹאשָׁהּ צָף עַל פְּנֵי הַמַּיִם.
(שולחן ערוך; יורה דעה, קצח:מ)

It is required that an adult (above age 12) Jewish woman supervise the immersing process. The main role prescribed in halacha for the *mikveh* attendant is to ensure that all hair is under the water. (It is also a good safety measure for preventing drowning.) The standard procedure at the *mikveh* is to stand unclothed before the *mikveh* attendant for final inspection prior to immersion, especially of hard to see places such as the back. However, the ultimate responsibility for *iyun* (checking) rests with the woman herself. Therefore, if the woman is careful and checks in a mirror, rechecking by another woman is not strictly required and there are halachically acceptable alternatives for those who feel uncomfortable with the usual procedure. For example, a woman who does not want her unclad body inpected by another can put on a robe and have the attendant check only her hands and feet. If even this arrangement is not acceptable to the woman, or if there is no Jewish female available to be the attendant, there are additional arrangements that can be made with rabbinic consultation.

---

[28] The reason for the ideal position is that in this way water will reach all the generally exposed parts during the immersion. By first wetting folds of the body that may not be exposed in a different position, however, a "connection" is formed with the water of the *mikveh*, and the immersion will be valid even if a particular fold is not exposed.

Blessing on immersion

כְּשֶׁפּוֹשֶׁטֶת מַלְבּוּשֶׁיהָ, כְּשֶׁעוֹמֶדֶת בַּחֲלוּקָה, תְּבָרֵךְ: "אֲשֶׁר קִדְּשָׁנוּ בְּמִצְוֹתָיו וְצִוָּנוּ עַל הַטְּבִילָה", וְתִפְשׁוֹט חֲלוּקָה וְתִטְבּוֹל; וְאִם לֹא בֵּרְכָה אָז, תְּבָרֵךְ לְאַחַר שֶׁתִּכָּנֵס עַד צַוָּארָהּ בַּמַּיִם; וְאִם הֵם צְלוּלִים, עוֹכַרְתָּן בְּרַגְלֶיהָ וּמְבָרֶכֶת. (שולחן ערוך; יורה דעה, ר)

וְיֵשׁ אוֹמְרִים שֶׁלֹּא תְּבָרֵךְ עַד אַחַר הַטְּבִילָה; וְכֵן נוֹהֲגִים שֶׁלְּאַחַר הַטְּבִילָה – בְּעוֹדָהּ עוֹמֶדֶת תּוֹךְ הַמַּיִם – מְכַסָּה עַצְמָהּ בְּבִגְדָהּ אוֹ בַחֲלוּקָה, וּמְבָרֶכֶת. (רמא; שם)

The blessing that is said is:

אֲשֶׁר קִדְּשָׁנוּ בְּמִצְוֹתָיו וְצִוָּנוּ עַל הַטְּבִילָה...

"...Who has sanctified us with His commandments and commanded us on immersion."

There is a disagreement between the *Shulchan Aruch* (Rav Yosef Caro, who represents the Sephardi tradition) and the *Rema* (Rav Moshe Isserles, who represents the Ashkenazi tradition) as to when this blessing should be said. The *Shulchan Aruch* maintains that a woman should say it before she immerses while she is still dressed, as is done with most blessings which are said prior to performing a commandment. The *Rema* maintains that she should make the blessing after immersion, so as not to differentiate from the immersion of a convert where the blessing is made after immersion (as before that he/she cannot say "Who... commanded us," as he/she is not yet Jewish). He states that she should cover herself with her robe while in the water and then make the blessing there. Although many Sephardim follow the practice of the Shulchan Aruch, and make the blessing before immersing while robed, the most common Ashkenazi custom is in fact neither of these.[29] Rather, the woman immerses herself once and makes the blessing in the water, with her head out of the water not looking down into the water. She then immerses one or

---

[29] *Shiurei Shevet Halevi, Hilchot Niddah* 200:6

more times, depending on her custom, after the blessing.[30] The water is considered to be enough of a covering that she can recite the blessing even while undressed. Some women also cross the arms below the heart to separate the upper body from the lower body.[31] Some women have the custom to cover their hair with a cloth while reciting this blessing.[32]

What is a proper *mikveh?*

For the cessation of the *niddah* status, one of two types of bodies of water can be used. These are known as *maayan* (a spring) and *mikveh* (a pool of rainwater).[33] Each of these must contain at least 40 *seah* of water (331 liters or approximately 87.5 US gallons[34]). The water also needs to cover the entire body at once, so that more would be needed for a large person. However, a small person can not use less than 40 *seah*). One of the differences between a *mikveh* and a *maayan* is that a *maayan* can be flowing water, while a *mikveh*'s water must be standing completely still and not flowing.

Other bodies of water may be used for immersion if they fit into one of these categories. An ocean is considered a *maayan*. However, beaches with access to the public often do not have secluded areas. A woman immersing under these conditions might rush in fear of being seen undressed, and thus not immerse properly. A river fed by spring water or melted ice water is also considered a *maayan*. Rivers can be used for immersion with the same caveats as those for the ocean. However, rivers whose source is mostly rainwater, or those that dry up during the summer months, are a form of *mikveh* and the fact that they flow (which is not permissible for a *mikveh*) is problematic. Similarly, artificial lakes can be problematic if they are accumulations of rainwater (thus a *mikveh*) and have run-off.[35]

---

[30] A woman should generally follow the custom of her mother. If there is no family custom, then one immersion prior to the blessing and one after the blessing is sufficient.

[31] Actually, the principle of לב רואה את הערוה does not apply to women, according to many opinions – see *Shach* and *Taz* on *Shulchan Aruch* YD 200. See also *Aruch Hashulchan* YD 200.

[32] Based on the *Ben Ish Chai*, year 2, *Parshat Shmini* 19.

[33] Here *mikveh* refers to the pool of rainwater, not to the building that houses it.

[34] Rav Chaim Naeh, *Sefer Shiurei Torah* 3:29. *Pinchas Even Yerushalayim*, 5707.

[35] *Aruch Hashulchan* 201.

Due to these considerations and others, the best choice for ritual immersion is a recognized and well-maintained constructed *mikveh*. When traveling or otherwise in a place with no official *mikveh*, other bodies of water can be used, but it must be determined that they meet halachic guidelines. One also must assure one's safety.

It should be pointed out that in the vast majority of *mikvaot*, the pool in which women immerse is not the accumulated rainwater but rather clean, chlorinated water. It has the ritual status of *mikveh* because it touches an adjacent pool of accumulated rainwater in a number of ritually acceptable ways (see Appendix D). The water of the immersion pool is changed frequently, often daily. Therefore, *mikvaot* are far cleaner than swimming pools and do not pose a health hazard. Women with health problems that require even greater caution, such as those undergoing chemotherapy, can arrange to be the first to use the *mikveh* after the water has been changed. If someone has a sensitivity to chlorine, even the small amount used in the *mikveh* water, special arrangements can be made in most *mikvaot* for immersion before the chlorine is added.

CHAPTER 5

EXPECTATION OF BEING *NIDDAH*

Times of separation *(onot prishah)* [1]

וְהִזַּרְתֶּם אֶת בְּנֵי יִשְׂרָאֵל מִטֻּמְאָתָם.. (ויקרא טו:לא)

You shall separate the children of Israel from their ritual impurity…

In order to minimize the risk that menstruation could begin during intercourse, relations are forbidden at the time a woman expects her menses. This practice is tied to the above cited verse, which indicates the need to distance oneself from the possibility of ritual impurity.

The time of a woman's expected menses is known as her *veset* (also known as *onot prishah*, times of separation). There are two basic categories of *veset*: those that depend on the date – *veset hayamim*, and those that depend on bodily sensations – *veset haguf*. During a *veset*, intercourse is forbidden but other forms of physical affection are allowed.[2]

---

[1] In the footnotes I mention more stringent customs which add further periods of separation beyond the actual <u>requirements</u> stated in the text. Some communities have adopted some of these customs, however, in which case they are binding on women of that community. A couple should discuss the additional stringencies between themselves – preferably with a rabbi. Note that it is halachically easier to add stringencies than to dispense with them subsequently.

[2] There are those with the custom to refrain from hugging and kissing as well.

Veset hayamim

בִּשְׁעַת וְסְתָּהּ, צָרִיךְ לִפְרוֹשׁ מִמֶּנָּה עוֹנָה אַחַת – וְלֹא מִשְּׁאָר קְרִיבוֹת אֶלָּא מִתַּשְׁמִישׁ
(הַמִּטָּה) בִּלְבָד. אִם הוּא בַּיּוֹם, פּוֹרֵשׁ מִמֶּנָּה אוֹתוֹ הַיּוֹם כּוּלוֹ אֲפִילוּ אִם הֶקֶּסֶת בְּסוֹפוֹ,
וּמוּתָּר מִיָּד בַּלַּיְלָה שֶׁלְּאַחֲרָיו ; וְכֵן אִם הוּא בִּתְחִלָּתוֹ, פּוֹרֵשׁ כָּל הַיּוֹם וּמוּתָּר כָּל הַלַּיְלָה
שֶׁלְּפָנָיו. וְכֵן הַדִּין אִם הוּא בַּלַּיְלָה, פּוֹרֵשׁ כָּל הַלַּיְלָה וּמוּתָּר בַּיּוֹם שֶׁלְּפָנָיו וְלִאֲחֲרָיו, בֵּין
שֶׁקָּבְעָה וֶסֶת בְּשָׁלֹשׁ פְּעָמִים אוֹ בְּפַעַם אַחַת. (שולחן ערוך ; יורה דעה, קפד:ב)

A *veset hayamim* is based on the calendar date of a woman's previous menstrual cycle. It is observed for one *onah* – either daytime (sunrise to sunset) or nighttime (sunset to sunrise) – corresponding to the onset of her most recent menses.

There are three basic times when most women have to anticipate their menses, based on the time they began to have uterine bleeding the previous cycle:

1. The same Hebrew date one month later
2. The interval between the last two times
3. The thirtieth day since the last time.

1. The same Hebrew date: וֶסֶת הַחוֹדֶשׁ

בִּרְאִיַּת הַיָּמִים, שֶׁהִיא לְיָמִים יְדוּעִים לַחוֹדֶשׁ, מִיָּד אַחַר שֶׁרָאֲתָה פַּעַם אַחַת לְיוֹם יָדוּעַ
לַחוֹדֶשׁ, כְּגוֹן כ״א אוֹ כ״ה בּוֹ, חוֹשֶׁשֶׁת לְפַעַם אֲחֶרֶת לְזֶה הַיּוֹם, וַאֲסוּרָה לְשַׁמֵּשׁ כָּל
אוֹתָהּ הָעוֹנָה. (שולחן ערוך ; יורה דעה, קפט:ב)

This is the same day of the Hebrew month *(chodesh)* and during the same *onah* (as defined above) as she began bleeding the previous month. For example, if her most recent menses began during the daytime of the 21st of *Tishrei,* she refrains from relations during the daytime on the 21st of *Cheshvan.*[3]

---

[3] If she began bleeding on the 30th of the month (the first day of a two-day *Rosh Chodesh*) and there are only 29 days in the next month, there is a dispute among halachic authorities. By most opinions, she would anticipate the first day (which is also *Rosh Chodesh*) of the following month. According to other opinions she does not keep a Hebrew date at all for that month.

2. The same interval: וֶסֶת הַפְלָגָה

מִיָּד אַחַר שֶׁרָאֲתָה פַּעַם אַחַת לְסוֹף עֶשְׂרִים חוֹשֶׁשֶׁת מִכָּאן וְאֵילָךְ כְּשֶׁיַּגִּיעַ עֶשְׂרִים.
(שולחן ערוך; יורה דעה, קפט:ב)

This is the interval (*haflagah*) between the last two times that she began her period. The day of onset of menses is counted both as the last day of the previous interval and the first day of the next interval. For example, she began her menses on the 25th of *Tevet*, and then again 26 days later on the 21st of *Shvat*. Counting the 21st of *Shvat* as day one of the next interval, her *veset* occurs 26 days later on the 16th of *Adar*.[4]

3. The thirtieth day: עוֹנָה בֵּינוֹנִית[5]

כָּל אִשָּׁה שֶׁאֵין לָהּ וֶסֶת קָבוּעַ, חוֹשֶׁשֶׁת לְיוֹם שְׁלוֹשִׁים לִרְאִיָּיתָהּ שֶׁהוּא עוֹנָה בֵּינוֹנִית לְסָתָם נָשִׁים. (שולחן ערוך; יורה דעה, קפט:א)

The "average" woman (the *beinonit*) is assumed to have intervals between periods of thirty days, calculated as described above. All women who have not established a permanent *veset* on a different day (as will be discussed below) halachically assume that they are like the average woman, and regard the thirtieth day as a time of anticipated menses.

וְעוֹנָה בֵּינוֹנִית, שֶׁהִיא לִשְׁלוֹשִׁים יוֹם, דִּינָהּ כְּוֶסֶת קָבוּעַ.
(שולחן ערוך; יורה דעה, קפט:ד)

Because this day is based on what is normal for "the general public" and not only for the particular woman, it has more stringent requirements in that she must do an internal exam during this *onah* to check whether in fact she began her menses; if she forgot to do an internal examination, she is not permitted to resume relations with her husband

---

4 Women who follow *Shulchan Aruch Harav* (Lubavitch) count the interval from the last day of bleeding to the first day of the next menses.

5 There are those who observe both the 30th and 31st day as *onah beinonit*.

until she does so.[6] However, if a woman forgot the internal examination on the Hebrew date or after the interval, she is not required to do one afterwards.

Thus, a woman who has no established pattern has to anticipate her period on three dates: the Hebrew date, the interval and the thirtieth day. At these times she should do at least one internal exam.[7] Often the Hebrew date and the *onah beinonit* coincide, in which case she observes only two *onot prishah*. This happens whenever the Hebrew lunar month is only 29 days long.

Sample calculations

Note: The following calendars are read from right to left.

Tevet

Sat	Fri	Thur	Wed	Tues	Mon	Sun
ב	א					
ט	# ח	# ז	# ו	# ה	# ד	ג
טז	טו	יד	יג	יב	יא	י
כג	כב	כא	כ	יט	יח	יז
	כט	כח	כז	כו	כה	כד

She bled on each day marked with a #, beginning on the 4th of *Tevet* at 10:00 am (the daytime *onah*), 28 days after the commencement of her menses the

---

[6] In addition, there are couples who separate only during the daytime or nighttime *onah* on other *veset* days, but observe a full 24-hour period of separation, from sunset to sunset, on the *onah beinonit*. This is in contradistinction to another custom, that of the *onah* of the *Or Zarua*. In that custom, an additional *onah* of separation is added BEFORE each veset.

[7] The basic requirement mentioned in the *Shulchan Aruch* is for one exam at some time during the anticipated *onah*. The *Chazon Ish*, 184:22, mentions two exams, one at the beginning and one at the end of the *onah*. *Sheuri Shevet Halevi* (184:9[4]) recommends three exams – at the beginning, middle and end of the *onah*. Even he agrees, however, that if the exams are painful one *bedikah* at the end of the *onah* is sufficient. However, if a woman forgot the internal examination on the Hebrew date or after the interval, she is not required to do one afterwards.

previous month. Her days of separation (*onot prishah*) for the following month, *Shvat*, are from sunrise to sunset on the following days:

1. The 4th of *Shvat* (the Hebrew date) (d)

2. The 2nd of *Shvat*, which is the 28th day (the interval) (i)

3. The 4th of *Shvat*, which is the 30th day (*onah beinonit*) (b)

Shvat

Sat	Fri	Thur	Wed	Tues	Mon	Sun
א						
ח	ז	# ו	# ה	# ד (d) (b)	# ג	ב (i)
טו	יד	יג	יב	יא	י	ט
כב	כא	כ	יט	יח	יז	טז
כט	כח	כז	כו	כה	כד	כג
						ל

Note that in this case there are only two *onot prishah*, as the *yom hachodesh* and *onah beinonit* overlap.

She started bleeding again on the 3rd of *Shvat* during the day, therefore the *onat prishah* of the 4th of *Shvat* fell during her days of *niddah*. Her *onot prishah* for the following month, *Adar*, are from sunrise to sunset on the following days:

1. The 3rd of *Adar* (the Hebrew date) (d)

2. The 1st of *Adar* (the interval – 29 days in this case)[8] (i)

3. The 2nd of Adar, which is the 30th day (*onah beinonit*) (b)

---

[8] Note that this was arrived at by counting the first day of bleeding as both the last day of the previous interval and the first day of the new interval.

Adar

Sat	Fri	Thur	Wed	Tues	Mon	Sun
ו#	ה#	ד#	ג (d)	ב (b)	א (i)	
יג	יב	יא	י	ט	ח	ז#
כ	יט	יח	יז	טז	טו	יד
כז	כו	כה	כד	כג	כב	כא
				ל	כט	כח

She started bleeding on Wednesday night after sunset, at the beginning of the 4th of *Adar*. In this case she kept all three *onot prishah*. Her days of anticipation for the following month, *Nisan*, are from sunset to sunrise on:

1. The 4th of *Nisan* (the Hebrew date)

2. The 5th of *Nisan* (the interval – 32 days in this case)

3. The 3rd of *Nisan* (the *onah beinonit*)

Establishing a *veset kavua*

וְלֹא אָמְרוּ שֶׁצָּרִיךְ לְקוֹבְעָם שָׁלֹשׁ פְּעָמִים אֶלָּא לְעִנְיַן עֲקִירָה, שֶׁכֵּיוָן שֶׁקּוֹבַעְתּוֹ בְּשָׁלֹשׁ פְּעָמִים אֵינוֹ נֶעֱקָר בְּפָחוֹת מִשָּׁלֹשׁ פְּעָמִים, שֶׁכָּל זְמַן שֶׁלֹּא עֲקָרַתּוּ שָׁלֹשׁ פְּעָמִים צְרִיכָה לָחוּשׁ לוֹ. אֲבָל לֵיאָסֵר, אֲפִילוּ בְּפַעַם אַחַת חוּשֶׁשֶׁת לוֹ פַּעַם שְׁנִיָּה. וּמִיהוּ אַף עַל פִּי שֶׁחוֹשֶׁשֶׁת לוֹ, נֶעֱקָר בְּפַעַם אַחַת, אֲפִילוּ קוֹבַעְתּוֹ שְׁתֵּי פְּעָמִים – שֶׁאִם רָאֲתָה שְׁנֵי יָמִים לְיוֹם יָדוּעַ, וּבַשְּׁלִישִׁית לֹא רָאֲתָה – אֵינָהּ חוֹשֶׁשֶׁת לוֹ עוֹד.

(שולחן ערוך; יורה דעה, קפט:ב)

עוֹד יֵשׁ חִילּוּק בֵּין קוֹבַעְתּוֹ שָׁלֹשׁ פְּעָמִים לְלֹא קוֹבַעְתּוֹ שָׁלֹשׁ פְּעָמִים: שֶׁהַקָּבוּעַ – אַף עַל פִּי שֶׁעָבְרָה עוֹנָתָהּ וְלֹא הִרְגִּישָׁה, אֲסוּרָה לְשַׁמֵּשׁ עַד שֶׁתִּבְדּוֹק וְתִמָּצֵא טְהוֹרָה. וְשֶׁלֹּא קוֹבַעְתּוֹ שָׁלֹשׁ פְּעָמִים – אִם הִגִּיעַ זְמַן הַוֶּסֶת וְלֹא בָּדְקָה וְלֹא רָאֲתָה, כֵּיוָן שֶׁעָבְרָה עוֹנָתָהּ, מוּתֶּרֶת. וְעוֹנָה בֵּינוֹנִית, שֶׁהִיא לִשְׁלֹשִׁים יוֹם, דִּינָהּ כְּוֶסֶת קָבוּעַ.

(שולחן ערוך; יורה דעה, קפט:ד)

Most women today, even those with what would medically be considered a regular period, expect their menses only within a given time range and not on a specific day. A few women, however, are able to predict the time of their menstruation exactly. Halachically, if a woman establishes a pattern of commencing her menses on the same Hebrew date or after the same interval three times in a row during the same *onah*,[9] she has what is called a *veset kavua* or established *veset*. A *veset kavua* has a number of implications, both lenient and stringent.

A woman with a *veset kavua* anticipates bleeding only on the day of the month or at the intervals she has established. She must do an internal examination during the *onah* of her *veset kavua*. If she forgot, she must do the examination before resuming relations with her husband.

If a woman with a *veset kavua* begins her menses on a day other than her *veset kavua*, then the following month she observes the Hebrew date and the interval from the deviant sighting, and also observes her *veset kavua*. She does not observe *onah beinonit*. If, for three consecutive cycles, she does not have bleeding on her *veset kavua*, the *veset kavua* is uprooted and she no longer anticipates it.

Even after a *veset kavua* has been uprooted, it remains dormant. Therefore, if she subsequently begins her menses in accordance with her former *veset kavua* – even one time – the *veset kavua* is immediately reestablished, even if years have passed since it was uprooted. Only if she she establishes a different *veset kavua* is her previous one permanently uprooted.

In addition to beginning to bleed on the same Hebrew date or after the same interval for three consecutive cycles, there are other ways of establishing a *veset kavua*; however, they are rare and rather complicated. If a woman notices any consistent pattern (such as bleeding on the same date every other month, or at gradually increasing or decreasing intervals), she should consult a rabbi to see if it meets the criteria of a one-time or an established *veset*. It is a good idea to keep a running list of the times and

---

[9] There are those who maintain that one can establish a *veset* of *haflagot* (intervals) with menses beginning at identical intervals from daytime to nighttime and from nighttime to daytime and so on.

dates of menstruation (such as that provided in Appendix F, p. 212), to allow for noticing potential patterns.

Veset haguf

יֵשׁ קוֹבַעַת וֶסֶת עַל יְדֵי מִקְרִים שֶׁיְּאָרְעוּ בְּגוּפָהּ כְּגוֹן:
שֶׁמְּפַהֶקֶת – דְּהַיְינוּ כְּאָדָם שֶׁפּוֹשֵׁט זְרוֹעוֹתָיו מֵחֲמַת כּוֹבֶד, אוֹ כְּאָדָם שֶׁפּוֹתֵחַ פִּיו מֵחֲמַת כּוֹבֶד, אוֹ שֶׁמּוֹצִיא קוֹל דֶּרֶךְ הַגָּרוֹן, וְכֵן אִם מִתְעַטֶּשֶׁת דֶּרֶךְ מַטָּה, אוֹ חוֹשֶׁשֶׁת בְּפִי כְרֵיסָהּ וּבְשִׁפּוּלֵי מֵעֶיהָ, אוֹ שֶׁאֲחָזוּהָ צִירֵי הַקַּדַּחַת, אוֹ שֶׁרֹאשָׁהּ וְאֵיבָרֶיהָ כְּבֵדִים עָלֶיהָ. בְּכָל אֶחָד מֵאֵלּוּ, אִם יָאָרַע לָהּ שָׁלֹשׁ פְּעָמִים, קָבְעָה לָהּ וֶסֶת, שֶׁבְּכָל פַּעַם שֶׁהִיא חוֹשֶׁשֶׁת מֵהֶם, אֲסוּרָה לְשַׁמֵּשׁ. וּמֵיהוּ, בִּפְהוּק אוֹ עִיטוּשׁ שֶׁל פַּעַם אֶחָד אֵין הַוֶּסֶת נִקְבָּע אֶלָּא כְּשֶׁעוֹשָׂה כֵן הַרְבֵּה פְּעָמִים זֶה אַחַר זֶה. וְאִם אֵירַע לָהּ שָׁלֹשׁ פְּעָמִים, שֶׁבְּכָל פַּעַם עָשְׂתָה כֵן הַרְבֵּה פְּעָמִים, הֲרֵי זֶה וֶסֶת. וְכָל אֵלּוּ הַוְּסָתוֹת שֶׁבְּגוּפָהּ אֵין לָהֶם זְמָן יָדוּעַ, אֶלָּא בְּכָל פַּעַם שֶׁיִּקְרֶה לָהּ זֶה זֶה הַמִּקְרֶה, הוּא וֶסֶת.
(שולחן ערוך ; יורה דעה, קפט:יט)

A woman can also anticipate menses and establish a *veset* based on bodily symptoms. The *Shulchan Aruch* lists a series of bodily sensations (which include those commonly reported by women as premenstrual symptoms[10]) which may signal the onset of menstruation. These symptoms have to be unique to her menses and to occur either with their onset or at a regular interval beforehand. As the rules of this are rather complicated, women should note any premenstrual symptoms and their proximity to the onset of menses. If a woman notices a pattern, she should consult an authority to determine if she can base her anticipation on these symptoms with or without other types of *veset*.

Women who do not have to observe the *onot prishah*

Certain women are presumed to be amenorrheic, and thus do not have to anticipate getting their period. These include those who are pregnant, those who are nursing and those who are postmenopausal.[11] The exact laws

---

[10] See Ganzel T and Zimmerman DR, *Veset Haguf – Hebet Refu'i Hilchati*, *Techumin* 5760; 20:363–75.

[11] The fourth category is a pre-pubertal girl. However, as girls today do not marry at that age, this has no practical significance today.

pertaining to each of these women will be discussed in the appropriate chapters in Part Three.

Bleeding caused by mechanical causes such as a medical exam, even if it renders her a *niddah*, does not require her to calculate days of anticipation from the time of the exam. In addition, days of anticipation are calculated only from the onset of actual bleeding and not from finding stains (other than on the *bedikah* cloth), even if the stains make her a *niddah* such as when they are larger than a *gris*. If she consistently stains at set intervals prior to her menses, she should consult with a rabbi to see if this would be considered a *veset haguf*.

If a woman never menstruates at less than 30-day intervals, she should discuss with a rabbi whether she needs to continue to keep all three *onot prishah*. The effect on the *onot prishah* of taking medication such as birth control pills is a matter of debate, and is further discussed in Part Four (pp. 167–168).

CHAPTER 6

COUPLE'S BEHAVIOR WHILE THE WIFE IS *NIDDAH*

Prohibited Activities

וְאֶל אִשָּׁה בְּנִדַּת טֻמְאָתָהּ לֹא תִקְרַב לְגַלּוֹת עֶרְוָתָהּ. (ויקרא יח:יט)

As mentioned in the introduction, a *niddah* is one of the *arayot*, women with whom sexual contact is forbidden. The grave punishment of *karet* applies to having sexual intercourse.[1] The verse about *niddah* states "you shall not approach." According to many opinions, this indicates a biblical prohibition against any form of intimate physical contact such as hugging and kissing (חִיבּוּק וְנִישׁוּק).[2] By rabbinic decree, other pleasurable physical interactions are forbidden as well.

Further distancing *(harchakot)*

חַיָּיב אָדָם לִפְרוֹשׁ מֵאִשְׁתּוֹ בִּימֵי טוּמְאָתָהּ עַד שֶׁתִּסְפּוֹר וְתִטְבּוֹל... וְלֹא יִשְׂחַק וְלֹא יָקֵל רֹאשׁ עִמָּהּ שֶׁמָּא יַרְגִּיל לַעֲבֵירָה; אֲבָל מוּתָּר לְהִתְיַיחֵד עִמָּהּ, דְּכֵיוָן שֶׁבָּא עָלֶיהָ פַּעַם אַחַת, תּוּ לֹא תָקֵיף יִצְרֵיהּ [שׁוּב לֹא תָּקֵיף יִצְרוֹ]. (שולחן ערוך; יורה דעה, קצה:א)

The case of a *niddah* is different than the other forbidden relationships in that it is a temporary situation. Intimacy for the same couple is at

---

[1] It should be stressed that the Biblical prohibition of sexual relations with a *niddah* and its attendant punishment of *karet* is independent of whether the couple is married or not.

[2] *Avot D'Rabbi Natan* 2:1, Rambam *Hilchot Isurei Biah* 21:1.

times forbidden and at times permitted. As the couple will be permitted to have physical relations after a period of time, we are not concerned about leaving them alone together, and thus there is no prohibition of a husband and wife who is a *niddah* being alone unchaperoned (*yichud*) (except for newlyweds who have not yet had intercourse for the first time.[3]) On the other hand, as the married couple have a certain level of familiarity and routine, there are additional prohibitions while the wife is a *niddah*, in order to prevent excessive intimacy that could lead to forbidden actions. These prohibitions are known as *harchakot*.

Husbands should realize that many women are embarrassed by what feels like a public declaration of the fact that they have their period. The seriousness of embarrassing a person needs to be balanced against the seriousness of *hilchot niddah*, and the couple should strive together to work out ways the *harchakot* can be observed discreetly.

כָּל אֵלּוּ הַהַרְחָקוֹת צָרִיךְ לְהַרְחִיק בֵּין בִּימֵי נִדּוּתָהּ בֵּין בִּימֵי לִיבוּנָהּ, שֶׁהֵם כָּל יְמֵי סְפִירָתָהּ ; וְאֵין חִילוּק בְּכָל אֵלּוּ בֵּין רוֹאָה מַמָּשׁ לְמוֹצֵאת כֶּתֶם.

(שולחן ערוך ; יורה דעה, קצה:יד)

Since a woman is a *niddah* until she immerses in the *mikveh*, these *harchakot* apply at all times until she immerses, even if she has ceased menstruating. They also apply to any situation that gave her *niddah* status, be it from biblical law or rabbinic decree. In some situations, certain activities are permitted to the husband but not to the wife, and vice versa. This comes from the rabbis' understanding of the differences between the sexes.

These prohibitions can be grouped into a number of categories:

Avoidance of all touching

לֹא יִגַּע בָּהּ אֲפִילוּ בְּאֶצְבַּע קְטַנָּה, וְלֹא יוֹשִׁיט מִיָּדוֹ לְיָדָהּ שׁוּם דָּבָר וְלֹא יְקַבְּלֶנּוּ מִיָּדָהּ, שֶׁמָּא יִגַּע בִּבְשָׂרָהּ.... (שולחן ערוך ; יורה דעה, קצה:ב)

---

[3] As further discussed in the Part Three – The Life Cycle (p. 117).

וְכֵן עַל יְדֵי זְרִיקָה מִיָּדוֹ לְיָדָהּ אוֹ לְהֵיפֶךְ, אָסוּר. (רמא ; שם)

There are safeguards to prevent any possibility of touching. Thus, passing things from hand to hand is forbidden. The gloss of the *Rema* extends this to throwing objects to each other as well. The couple should not sit so close together that it is inevitable that they will touch. Based on the gloss of the *Rema* to *Yoreh Deah* 195:5, Ashkenazic custom further proscribes sitting on the same seat if it is a moving seat (such as a swing), or if the weight of one person will be felt by the other (such as a soft couch). The couple can sit on the same seat if an object or person is placed in between them.

Eating together

The *Shulchan Aruch* states:

לֹא יֹאכַל עִמָּהּ עַל הַשֻּׁלְחָן אֶלָּא אִם כֵּן יֵשׁ שׁוּם שִׁינוּי שֶׁיִּהְיֶה שׁוּם דָּבָר מַפְסִיק בֵּין קְעָרָה שֶׁלּוֹ לִקְעָרָה שֶׁלָּהּ, לֶחֶם אוֹ קַנְקַן, אוֹ שֶׁיֹּאכַל כָּל אֶחָד בְּמַפָּה שֶׁלּוֹ. (שולחן ערוך ; יורה דעה, קצה : ג)

To understand this *harchakah*, one needs only to think about a romantic candlelit dinner at a table for two. This can lead to a degree of intimacy that is not desired during this time period. The couple should not eat next to each other at the same table without some form of reminder of her forbidden status. This can be separate placemats, or some inanimate object placed between them that is not moved during the meal. It should be a private signal between the couple and should not be obvious to others in the room. There are some opinions that this prohibition applies when they are eating alone, but not in the presence of other adults or children old enough to cause embarrassment.[4] This can be relied upon if a signal could lead to embarrassment.

יֵשׁ אוֹמְרִים שֶׁאָסוּר לוֹ לֶאֱכֹל מִשְׁיוּרֵי מַאֲכָל שֶׁלָּהּ, כְּמוֹ שֶׁאָסוּר לִשְׁתּוֹת מִשְׁיוּרֵי כּוֹס שֶׁלָּהּ. (רמא ; יורה דעה, קצה : ג)

---

[4] *Pitchei Teshuvah* 195:5.

As a couple cannot, in unlimited fashion, share a table, all the more so they may not eat off the same plate – a situation that is common, for instance, at a smorgasbord. A corollary of this principle of not eating from the same plate is that the husband cannot eat food his wife has left over.

לֹא יִשְׁתֶּה מִשְּׁיּוּרֵי כּוֹס שֶׁשָּׁתְתָה הִיא. (שולחן ערוך ; יורה דעה, קצה:ד)

אִם לֹא שֶׁמַּפְסִיק אָדָם אַחֵר בֵּינֵיהֶם, אוֹ שֶׁהוּרַק מִכּוֹס זֶה אֶל כּוֹס אַחֵר (אֲפִילוּ הוּחְזַר לְכוֹס) ; וְאִם שָׁתְתָה וְהוּא אֵינוֹ יוֹדֵעַ, וְרוֹצֶה לִשְׁתּוֹת מִכּוֹס שֶׁלָּהּ – אֵינָהּ צְרִיכָה לְהַגִּיד לוֹ שֶׁלֹּא יִשְׁתֶּה. וְהִיא מוּתֶּרֶת לִשְׁתּוֹת מִכּוֹס שֶׁשָּׁתָה הוּא. וְאִם שָׁתְתָה מִכּוֹס וְהָלְכָה לָהּ, יֵשׁ אוֹמְרִים שֶׁמּוּתָּר לוֹ לִשְׁתּוֹת הַמּוּתָר, דִּמְאַחַר שֶׁכְּבָר הָלְכָה אֵין כָּאן חִבָּה. (רמא ; שם)

This applies not only to leftover food, but also to leftover drink. In the case of drink, the husband can have the remainder of his wife's beverage under any one of the following conditions:

1. Someone else has drunk from the cup in between.

2. The liquid was transferred from cup to cup (even if then put back in the original cup).

3. He doesn't know that she has drunk from this cup (and she does not have to go out of her way to tell him).

4. She is no longer in the vicinity.

The wife can drink after her husband at any time without additional conditions.

Sharing a bed

לֹא יֵשֵׁב בַּמִּטָּה הַמְיֻחֶדֶת לָהּ, אֲפִילוּ שֶׁלֹּא בְּפָנֶיהָ. (שולחן ערוך ; יורה דעה, קצה:ה)

As there are obvious romantic associations to the bedroom, the *Shulchan Aruch* states that a husband should not sit on his wife's bed when she is a *niddah* even if she is not present. There is a debate among authorities as to actual practice. The *Shach* quotes the *Bach* who makes a distinction between sitting and lying down. According to him, the husband may not lie on his wife's bed at any time when she is *niddah*. However, to sit there for a short period such as while getting dressed is permitted. The *Taz* forbids any form of sitting or lying by the husband. The wife may sit on her husband's bed if he is in the room but she may not lie down. If he is absent, she may sit or lie on his bed. A couple should consult with their rabbi as to how to conduct themselves.

לֹא יִישַׁן עִמָּהּ בְּמִטָּה, אֲפִילוּ כָל אֶחָד בְּבִגְדּוֹ וְאֵין נוֹגְעִין זֶה בָּזֶה.
(שולחן ערוך ; יורה דעה, קצה:ו)

וַאֲפִילוּ יֵשׁ לְכָל אֶחָד מַצָּע בִּפְנֵי עַצְמוֹ, וַאֲפִילוּ אִם שׁוֹכְבִים בִּשְׁתֵּי מִטּוֹת וְהַמִּטּוֹת
נוֹגְעוֹת זוֹ בָּזוֹ – אָסוּר. (רמא ; שם)

The couple may not sleep on the same bed even if they are fully clothed, covered with different blankets and not touching. For this reason most couples have two different beds which can be brought together when relations are permitted and separated when they are not. Other arrangements such as a king size bed and a trundle, or one bed and a sleep couch can be used if the couple wishes.

Dress

לֹא יִסְתַּכֵּל אֲפִילוּ בַּעֲקֵבָהּ וְלֹא בִּמְקוֹמוֹת הַמְּכוּסִּים שֶׁבָּהּ.
(שולחן ערוך ; יורה דעה, קצה:ז)
אֲבָל מוּתָּר לְהִסְתַּכֵּל בָּהּ בִּמְקוֹמוֹת הַגְּלוּיִים אַף עַל פִּי שֶׁנֶּהֱנֶה בִּרְאִיָּיתָהּ. (רמא ; שם)

The husband should not gaze at the parts of his wife's body that are generally covered. Parts normally uncovered such as her face are not forbidden, even if he enjoys looking at them.

There is debate among the authorities as to whether hair counts as a covered part of the body, since married women cover their hair when they go out. Rav Moshe Feinstein[5] states that if she generally has her hair uncovered in the house, her husband is used to seeing it and it does not have to be covered in the house when she is a *niddah*.

רְאוּיָה לָהּ שֶׁתְּיַיחֵד לָהּ בְּגָדִים לִימֵי נִדּוּתָהּ, כְּדֵי שֶׁיִּהְיוּ שְׁנֵיהֶם זוֹכְרִים תָּמִיד שֶׁהִיא נִדָּה. (שולחן ערוך ; יורה דעה, קצה:ח)

At a time in history when it was important for everyone to know if a woman was a *niddah* due to its effect on the ritual purity of foods, women wore special, less valuable clothes while they had the status of *niddah*.[6] While this is no longer required, some continue the practice in a quiet way as another reminder to each other of her current status.

The wife should not go out of her way to be enticing while a *niddah*. However, as the halacha certainly does not want the couple to be turned off to each other, she can continue to dress to be attractive.

Signs of affection

The Talmud[7] lists three chores a wife normally performs for her husband, that are considered to have special overtones of affection. These are pouring wine, making a bed and drawing a bath. Due to these overtones, they should not be done in their usual way while she is a *niddah*.

a. pouring a drink

כָּל מְלָאכוֹת שֶׁהָאִשָּׁה עוֹשָׂה לְבַעְלָהּ, נִדָּה עוֹשָׂה לוֹ – חוּץ מִמְּזִיגַת הַכּוֹס, שֶׁאֲסוּרָה לִמְזוֹג הַכּוֹס [בְּפָנָיו] וּלְהַנִּיחוֹ לְפָנָיו עַל הַשֻּׁלְחָן אֶלָּא אִם כֵּן תַּעֲשֶׂה שׁוּם הֶיכֵּר : כְּגוֹן, שֶׁתַּנִּיחֶנּוּ עַל הַשֻּׁלְחָן בְּיַד שְׂמֹאל, אוֹ תַּנִּיחֶנּוּ עַל הַכַּר אוֹ עַל הַכֶּסֶת אֲפִילוּ בְּיַד יְמִינָהּ. (שולחן ערוך ; יורה דעה, קצה:י)

---

[5] YD 2:75.

[6] In the days before modern underwear or sanitary napkins this probably had practical reasons as well, so that all one's good clothes were not ruined.

[7] *Ketubot* 61a.

A *niddah* should not pour a drink for her husband in his presence and place it in front of him, unless she signals that things are different, e.g., using her left hand or putting the cup on a chair rather then the table.

כְּשֵׁם שֶׁאֲסוּרָה לִמְזוֹג לוֹ, כָּךְ הוּא אָסוּר לִמְזוֹג לָהּ ; וְלֹא עוֹד, אֶלָּא אֲפִילוּ לִשְׁלוֹחַ לָהּ כּוֹס שֶׁל יַיִן אָסוּר – לֹא שָׁנָא [מְשַׁנֶּה] כּוֹס שֶׁל בְּרָכָה לֹא שָׁנָא כּוֹס אַחֵר – אִם הוּא מְיוּחָד לָהּ ; אֲבָל אִם שׁוֹתִים הֵם מֵאוֹתוֹ הַכּוֹס וְשָׁתַית אִיהִי אַבָּתְרַיְיהוּ, לֵית לַן בַּהּ [וּשְׁתִיָּה שֶׁלָּהּ הִיא אַחֲרָיו, אֵין לָנוּ בָהּ אִיסוּר]. (שולחן ערוך ; יורה דעה, קצה :יג)

The husband should also not pour specifically for his wife, nor directly pass her a cup of wine. Thus, after making *kiddush* he may fill a number of cups and pass them around the table, and his wife may take any cup when the tray gets to her. Alternatively, he can place the *kiddush* cup on the table and she can pick it up.

b. making a bed

אֲסוּרָה לְהַצִּיעַ מִטָּתוֹ בְּפָנָיו – וְדַוְקָא פְּרִיסַת סְדִינִים וְהַמִּכְסֶה שֶׁהוּא דֶרֶךְ חִבָּה – אֲבָל הַצָּעַת הַכָּרִים וְהַכְּסָתוֹת שֶׁהוּא טוֹרַח וְאֵינָה דֶרֶךְ חִבָּה, שְׁרֵי [מוּתָּר]. וְשֶׁלֹּא בְּפָנָיו – הַכֹּל מוּתָּר, אֲפִילוּ הוּא יוֹדֵעַ שֶׁהִיא מַצַּעַת אוֹתָם. (שולחן ערוך ; יורה דעה, קצה :יא)

She should not make his bed in his presence. This does not apply to the chore of putting on the sheet or pillow case, but to the more affectionate, careful arrangement of the bed such as "turn down service." Not in his presence, this too is permitted.

c. drawing a bath

אֲסוּרָה לִיצוֹק לוֹ מַיִם לִרְחוֹץ פָּנָיו יָדָיו וְרַגְלָיו, אֲפִילוּ אֵינָה נוֹגַעַת בּוֹ וַאֲפִילוּ הֵם מַיִם צוֹנְנִים. (שולחן ערוך ; יורה דעה, קצה :יב)

She should not pour water for him to wash his hands, face and feet even if she does not directly touch him and even if it is not warm water. The modern example would be preparing a bath.

Frivolous behavior

וְלֹא יִשְׂחֹק וְלֹא יָקֵל רֹאשׁ עִמָּהּ שֶׁמָּא יַרְגִּיל לַעֲבֵירָה.
(שולחן ערוך; יורה דעה, קצה:א)

In addition to those things clearly spelled out, any other actions that are liable to lead to intimacy should be avoided during this time period. Frivolous talk or behavior is frowned upon. This does not preclude being friendly – something husbands should seriously consider, as women often feel "unloved" at this point, especially because of the constant reminder of their *niddah* status engendered by *harchakot*. Thoughtful gestures – sending letters or cards, small gifts, flowers for Shabbat – can help counterbalance this negative message.

When one of the couple is ill

אִם הוּא חוֹלֶה וְאֵין לוֹ מִי שֶׁיְּשַׁמְּשֶׁנּוּ זוּלָתָהּ, מוּתֶּרֶת לְשַׁמְּשׁוֹ – רַק שֶׁתִּזָּהֵר בְּיוֹתֵר שֶׁתּוּכַל מֵהַרְחָצַת פָּנָיו יָדָיו וְרַגְלָיו וְהַצָעַת הַמִּטָּה בְּפָנָיו.
(שולחן ערוך; יורה דעה, קצה:טו)

אִשָּׁה חוֹלָה וְהִיא נִדָּה, אָסוּר לְבַעֲלָהּ לִיגַּע בָּהּ כְּדֵי לְשַׁמְּשָׁהּ: כְּגוֹן, לְהָקִימָהּ וּלְהַשְׁכִּיבָהּ וּלְסָמְכָהּ. (שולחן ערוך; יורה דעה, קצה:טז)

וְיֵשׁ אוֹמְרִים דְּאִם אֵין לָהּ מִי שֶׁיְּשַׁמְּשֶׁנָּה, מוּתָּר בַּכֹּל; וְכֵן נוֹהֲגִין אִם צְרִיכָה הַרְבֵּה לְכָךְ. (רמא; שם)

When the husband is ill and there is no one else to assist, his wife who is a *niddah* may do what is needed to care for him. However, she should avoid touching him and doing those tasks that the halacha considers particularly affectionate. The rules are more stringent when she is ill than when he is, as when he is ill he is unlikely to initiate sexual contact. When she is ill, he should be particularly careful not to touch her, if possible, or else to touch her only on her clothes or while wearing gloves. Allowing her to suffer when she really needs his help is not an option.[8] Furthermore, when the situation is one of life or death, saving life, of course, overrides these considerations.

---

[8] *Darchei Moshe* 195:6.

PART TWO

PRACTICAL GUIDE AND REVIEW

"A time to embrace and a time to refrain from embracing"[1] well describes the physical relationship outlined by Jewish law between a husband and wife. During the time that the wife has the halachic status of *niddah*, no physical contact between a couple is permitted, as will be further explained below. Much has been written explaining the philosophy behind this practice[2] and will not be repeated here. This part focuses on how to observe these *halachot*, and not why.

This section is meant as review. Therefore, those who have already read Part One will find most things repeated here. However, the questions and answers at the end of the section are original. Those who are starting with Part Two, will find that the points discussed are further elucidated in Part One.

---

[1] Ecclesiastes 3:5

[2] See for example, R. Slonim, *Total Immersion: A Mikvah Anthology* (Northvale, New Jersey: Aronson, 1997; revised edition from Urim Publications, 2006).

CHAPTER 1

CAUSES OF THE *NIDDAH* STATUS

The following situations lead to the onset of the *niddah* status:

A: Bleeding

The only bleeding that makes a woman a *niddah* is uterine bleeding. Bleeding not of a uterine source, such as vaginal irritation, does not make her a *niddah*. Similarly, other bleeding in the genital area such as from a rectal fissure does not make a woman a *niddah*.

From the halachic standpoint, bleeding refers to discharge of shades of either red or black. Other colors of uterine discharge such as white (physiologic leukorrhea) and green, are completely permissible. Bright or light yellow is permissible. Darker yellow shades may be problematic in some circumstances. Oranges, tans, and browns need to be shown to a rabbi to determine if they are too close to red or black.[1]

---

[1] This is probably the area of *hilchot niddah* that makes women most uncomfortable – Show my underwear to a Rabbi?! However, this is generally for the woman's benefit. Many colors that women consider problematic are in fact permissible, and thus a couple need be physically separated for shorter periods of time. This is particularly true for brownish discharges at the end of one's menstrual flow, where refraining from asking can add a number of unnecessary days to the process. Some women feel they are being "more careful" by not asking and just waiting, but in this area of halacha this is not true. There is no obligation to be a *niddah* longer than necessary, and a couple's being separated limits their opportunities to perform other commandments such as procreation and marital relations *(onah)*.

Whether or not a woman has a sensation determines whether her *niddah* status is biblical or rabbinic. While the same laws generally apply to both, the distinction can occasionally be important. The halachically relevant sensations are:

1. Her whole body shakes

2. She feels her uterus open

3. She feels liquid flowing within the reproductive tract.

If she had any of these sensations – a relatively rare occurrence for most women – she should do an internal examination (*bedikah*). If she finds a discharge of a forbidden color, she is a *niddah*. If she finds a discharge of a permissible color she can attribute the sensation to that discharge, and she is still permitted to her husband. If she does not find anything she should consult a rabbi, as there are some circumstances that would result in her being a *niddah*.

External dampness is not a halachically relevant sensation. Neither are backaches, nausea or other premenstrual symptoms, but they may be a precursor of expected menses (*veset*). (See chapter 3, p. 97)

There are also situations in which we are concerned lest she had a sensation but attributed it to something else. These situations are:

In time, one can become comfortable in approaching a rabbi with these questions directly, similar to the way one tends to become more comfortable with gynecologist visits and exams.

There are also ways to circumvent direct contact with the rabbi, such as sending cloths for examination and then asking about them over the telephone. Most rabbis are willing to answer these questions anonymously if desired. If the woman is uncomfortable, she can ask her husband to go to the rabbi instead. It should be pointed out, however, that direct discussion with the rabbi allows more factors to be taken into consideration in answering questions and thus a more accurate assessment can be made. Nishmat, The Jeanie Schottenstein Center for Advanced Torah Study for Women, trains "Yoatzot Halacha" – women trained to be a first address in these intimate questions and assist women not willing or able to turn directly to a rabbi. They are accessible through a hotline (toll free 1-877-YOETZET (1-877-963-8938) from the United States and Canada, +972-2-640-4343 from elsewhere) and a website, www.yoatzot.org.

1. urination

2. sexual intercourse

3. internal examination.

Therefore, if she sees blood immediately after urination or intercourse, or sees blood on the cloth she used for an internal examination, the halacha is more stringent, as she may have had a sensation that she did not notice.

B: External stains

Even in the absence of any sensation, stains of a forbidden color found on the body or external surfaces can still induce the *niddah* state on a rabbinic level, subject to certain conditions:

> **1. Size**. If the stain is less than the size of a *gris* (the area of a circle 19 millimeters (about ¾ inch) in diameter), it does not make her a *niddah*. If there are a number of small stains near each other, they are measured individually if found on clothing, but are added together if found on her body.

> **2. Type of surface**. Stains found on substances that cannot acquire ritual impurity do not make her a *niddah*. Common examples are the toilet seat, the ground and, according to most opinions, toilet paper.

> **3. Color of the garment**. If a stain is found on a cloth or surface that is a color other than white or light beige, she is generally not a *niddah* based on this stain alone.

> **4. Location**. Only stains found in places where they could conceivably have come from the uterus render her a *niddah*. Thus stains found on her legs are problematic, but those on her upper arms are not.

5. An alternative explanation. If she can reasonably attribute the stain to some other source such as a cut or wound on her body or her having dealt with bloody objects such as in the kitchen or in a laboratory, it would not make her a *niddah*.

According to Ashkenazi custom, the rules for attributing a stain to an external source are more stringent during the first three of the seven blood-free days. Thus, during this period, if she is not *positive* that the blood is from the external source she should ask a rabbinic question.

C: Statement that she is *niddah*

If a woman states she is a *niddah,* she is considered a *niddah* (even if she actually is not) and has to count the requisite days and immerse in the *mikveh,*[2] unless she has a reasonable explanation why she said so incorrectly.

D: Childbirth

A vaginal birth (or spontaneous or induced abortion more than 40 days after conception) makes a woman a *yoledet* in addition to being a *niddah*. In the unlikely event that she ceased bleeding within five days after normal childbirth,[3] she could thus go to the *mikveh* twelve days after birth if she had a boy, but for a girl she has to wait until after the minimum 14 days prescribed in the Torah. Almost always, however, bleeding after birth continues for a number of weeks. When she ceases staining and counts seven blood-free days as described below, she can immerse in the *mikveh*.

E: Hymenal bleeding

Although the bleeding that may accompany the stretching of the hymen the first time a virgin has intercourse is NOT uterine bleeding, she assumes the status of *niddah* by Rabbinic decree. The newlyweds complete the first act of intercourse in normal fashion, in spite of the flow of hymenal blood. After this, however – even if there was no visible bleeding – they separate

---

[2] Although in this case she immerses without a blessing.

[3] Short bleeding is more possible after a miscarriage. If the sex of the miscarried or aborted fetus is not known, one waits 14 days as if it were female.

for a minimum of 11 days (rather than the usual twelve, as explained below) – four days until she can begin to count[4] and then seven blood-free days. During this time they have to observe all the separations required when the wife is a *niddah*.

If she was a *niddah* at the time of marriage or if her menses commenced prior to their first intercourse, the newlyweds may not be alone together. If the situation arises, a rabbi should be consulted as to how best to handle the practical implications of this. These implications are an additional reason that exta care is taken when setting the wedding date as will be discussed in detail in Part Three (pp.117–118).

F: Medical procedures

Medical procedures that lead to opening of the cervix more than a minimal amount (opinions for this amount vary between authorities) cause the onset of the *niddah* status even in the absence of evident bleeding. Full discussion of this topic is found in Part Four, chapter 1 (pp.144–145).

---

[4] In this case, Ashkenazim also wait four days rather than five.

CHAPTER 2

THE CESSATION OF THE *NIDDAH* STATUS

Seven clean days *(shiva neki'im)*

All women must count seven blood-free days before going to the *mikveh*. Even if bleeding stopped after one or two days, she cannot start to count seven days until four days (for many Sephardim) or five days (for Ashkenazim) have passed from the onset of bleeding.

In order to verify that she has in fact stopped bleeding, a woman has to do an internal exam. This exam is called a *hefsek taharah.* (Such an exam at other times is known as a *bedikah.*) It is done as follows:

> She takes a white, pre-checked soft cotton cloth, wraps it around her finger, and inserts it deeply but GENTLY into the vaginal canal. She then moves her finger circumferentially around the vaginal canal, GENTLY touching the sides, being careful to enter the crevices of the vaginal canal. She then withdraws the cloth and checks it in a good light. If all discharge on the cloth is white, clear, or light yellow, her bleeding is assumed to have stopped and she can count the NEXT day as the first of her seven blood free days. If it is obviously red, then she will need to try again. If it is any other color she should have it shown to an authority who is knowledgeable in this field.

The *hefsek taharah* must be done during the daylight hours, preferably late in the day, shortly before sunset. Prior to the *hefsek taharah,* she should clean the external vaginal area. Busy women who may be occupied (especially on short winter afternoons) and don't find these exams painful or troublesome should consider doing one in the morning and repeating it before sunset. In this way they have a "backup" in case of forgetting. On *erev Shabbat* she should check before candlelighting; however, as long as she checks before sunset the exam is valid.

Following the *hefsek taharah*, the custom is to use a *moch dachuk* – literally, closely packed wadding. This involves packing the vagina from sunset to nightfall. This is generally done by taking one or two *bedikah* cloths and inserting them into the vaginal canal. Some authorities permit the use of a tampon instead. It is a good idea to sit or lie down during this period, to prevent irritation of the vaginal wall that can cause stains from vaginal rather than uterine blood. Women who find this exam uncomfortable should consult a rabbi. If she made a *hefsek taharah* but forgot the *moch dachuk*, in most cases she may nevertheless count the next day as the first of the seven clean days.[1]

The seven blood-free days begin the day AFTER she does her *hefsek taharah* (the 24-hour Jewish day begins with the previous night).[2] During these days, a woman needs to ascertain that bleeding has not restarted. For this purpose, women used to wear white clothes and use white linens (hence these seven blood free days are known as her white days). However, now that many women wear form fitting underpants, it is no longer necessary to wear white clothes; white underwear is sufficient. Women who wear white underwear to sleep may also omit the white sheets.[3] If white underwear is unavailable, she does not need to delay counting the seven blood-free days; she can wear clean prechecked undergarments of another color until white becomes available.

A woman furthermore ascertains that bleeding has not restarted by doing internal examinations, known *as bedikot*. The procedure is the same as that for the *hefsek taharah*. Ideally, a woman performs two internal examina-

---

[1] The exception is when the *hefsek taharah* is performed on the same day she began bleeding.

[2] Assuming that the four or five day minimum has passed

[3] Some women still keep the custom of white sheets. Others are embarrassed by people knowing what status they are in.

tions per day (*bedikot*), one in the morning after sunrise and one in the afternoon before sunset. However, if the exams are painful, uncomfortable, or she feels she is irritating herself she should speak to a rabbi as to how to reduce the number.

If she missed one out of the two daily exams, she should continue to check as usual the next day. If she forgot both exams on one of the intermediate days, she should continue to check as usual the next day. Days one and seven are essential, however, and every effort must be made not to forget or miss these exams; if missed, a rabbi must be consulted. Fortunately, these days are easy to remember: day one is the day after the *hefsek taharah*, and day seven is the day after which she will go to the *mikveh* in the evening.

(For examples of counting, see Part One, pp.46–48 and in Frequently Asked Questions at the end of this section, pp.105–108.)

Mikveh use

The end of bleeding and the counting of seven blood-free days are necessary for the cessation of the *niddah* status, but are not sufficient. Even if years have gone by since her last menses, a woman retains her status of *niddah*, with all its attendant prohibitions, until she immerses properly in a proper *mikveh*.

Preparation

Immersion requires that the entire body be under water at the same time. Thus, if there was any impediment or barrier *(chatzitzah)* between any part of the body and the water, one has to remove the *chatzitzah* and then re-immerse the entire body. Every effort must be made in advance to remove even miniscule barriers. If a barrier was overlooked and discovered after immersion, a rabbi should be consulted, as not every impediment requires re-immersion after the fact.

Determining that there are no barriers to immersion involves a two-part process: first, cleansing to remove any possible barrier, and second, inspection to verify that all barriers have in fact been removed.

Cleansing

Cleansing can be divided into a number of steps:

1. Removing obviously foreign material – clothing, rings, necklaces, earrings and other jewelry, contact lenses.[4]

2. Washing hair with warm water.[5] This is known as *chafifah*. Hair in itself is not a *chatzitzah*, but as there is an opinion that anything that is about to be removed is a *chatzitzah*, if she intends to remove hair (e.g., to shave her legs or underarms) she should do so before and not after immersing. Knots in the hair are a form of *chatzitzah*, and must be removed or combed out. Hair on the head is combed with a comb; for other hair such as pubic or axillary, separating the strands with fingers is sufficient.

3. Washing the entire body with water. Preferably this is done with warm water. However, if there is a shortage of warm water, the body can be washed in cold water and the warm water saved for the hair, where use of warm water is essential. While this washing is generally done by bathing in a bathtub, a shower is acceptable, as long as one is careful to wash the entire body.

4. Certain parts of the body require special attention such as the armpits, under the breasts and other crevices known as *beit hastarim*, "the hidden places." The mouth also falls under this category. Therefore, teeth and gums must be thoroughly cleaned by brushing and flossing to remove any trapped particles of food, although there is no obligation to let water enter the mouth during immersion.

---

[4] Even if water can permeate the item, if the woman is concerned lest the item be ruined, it is a *chatzitzah*, according to most opinions.

[5] Shampoo can be used to assure that the hair is clean. Some conditioners that leave a film on the hair may be problematic.

5. Using the bathroom before immersion is recommended. Nevertheless, if she forgot to do so, this does not invalidate the immersion.

6. Dirt beneath nails is a form of *chatzitzah*, and the custom is to cut nails short. However, the nails themselves are not a *chatzitzah*, and thus if she has a professional or emotional need for her long nails, this is allowed, as long as they are well cleaned.[6]

7. Makeup and nail polish should be removed. If she has permanent makeup, hair dye or a well maintained manicure that she does not want to remove, she should consult a rabbi.

8. Bandages should be removed. In the case of items that cannot be removed for medical reasons, such as stitches, she should consult a rabbi.

Cleansing can be done either at home or in the preparation rooms available at the *mikveh*. If done at home, she should comb her hair again at the *mikveh* (if it is not Shabbat or *Yom Tov*) and wet her body before immersion (a quick shower is sufficient).

There is a disagreement about the ideal timing of *chafifah*. According to one opinion, it is best to do it at night immediately prior to immersion. According to the other, it is best to do it in the daytime, for if she waits until nighttime, she may be in a rush to get home and not do it properly. The custom is to follow both opinions by starting *chafifah* during the day and continuing into the night. However, if circumstances (work, young children, unavailability of water) preclude one option, the other is acceptable.

---

[6] Sometimes a particular *mikveh* may have firm rules about adhering to the custom of cutting nails short. A women who plans to immerse with long nails should clarify this issue in advance.

At times, one option or the other is precluded for halachic reasons. Washing hair is not permitted on Shabbat or *Yom Tov*, so if a woman goes to the *mikveh* Friday night she must prepare during the day on Friday. If she goes to the *mikveh* Saturday night, on the other hand, she cannot prepare during the day on Shabbat. According to some opinions, she should do some preparation during the day on Friday and repeat it on Saturday night. In all circumstances, inspection is required just prior to immersing.

Inspection

All parts of the body that she can see by herself should be visually inspected. All other parts should be felt to ensure that there is no foreign material. *Chafifah* of the head is a form both of cleansing and of inspection.

Timing

Immersion takes place at night after the completion of the seven blood-free days. Even if a woman immerses on a later date, she needs to immerse at night. In extreme circumstances, such as if the *mikveh* is in an area that is unsafe at night, she may be permitted to go during daylight hours on the eighth or subsequent days. A rabbi should be consulted.

If both members of the couple are in town, the woman should go to the *mikveh* on the earliest permitted night. Doing so enables a couple to perform two commandments – procreation and marital relations. If one member of the couple is away, there are differences of opinion as to whether it is preferable to immerse on time or to wait for the spouse to return.

Procedure

One enters the water until the entire body is under water. The ideal position is slightly crouched, hands extended, fingers slightly apart, eyes and mouth closed gently – in such a position that all parts of the body and all her hair are under the water. The minimum is one immersion. Customs vary on how many additional dunkings are done. There is a difference in custom between Sephardim, who make the blessing before entering the water, and Ashkenazim, who make the blessing while in the water, generally after the first immersion.

The bracha that is said is:

...אֲשֶׁר קִדְּשָׁנוּ בְּמִצְוֹתָיו וְצִוָּנוּ עַל הַטְּבִילָה.

"...who has sanctified us with His commandments and commanded us on immersion."

An adult (above age 12) Jewish woman should supervise the immersion to insure that all the hair is covered by the water. (It is also a good safety measure to avoid drowning.) This is the main purpose of the "*mikveh* lady." Furthermore, she can verify that any *chatzitzah* has been removed from hard to see places such as one's back.

The best place for ritual immersion is in a known and well-maintained *mikveh*. When traveling, or otherwise in a place with no official *mikveh*, natural bodies of water such as seas and rivers can often be used, but a rabbi should be consulted about the details.

CHAPTER 3

EXPECTATION OF BEING *NIDDAH*

Times of separation

Relations are forbidden at the time of anticipated menses, to prevent them
from inadvertently coinciding with the onset of the *niddah* status. This time
of expected menses is known as her *veset*. During this time, intercourse is
forbidden but other forms of intimacy are allowed.[1] There are two basic
categories of *veset*: those that depend on the date – *veset hayamim* – and those
that depend on bodily sensations – *veset haguf*.

Veset hayamim

This is the portion of the day (either sunrise to sunset or sunset to sunrise)
called an *onah*, corresponding to when she had started menstruating in the
past.

There are three days when women have to anticipate their menses
based on the time they began their previous menstrual cycle: on the same
date of the Hebrew month, after an interval which is the same as that
which elapsed between the last two cycles, and on the thirtieth day from
the last cycle.

---

[1] There are those who also refrain from hugging and kissing.

The same Hebrew date: *veset hachodesh*

This is the same date of the Hebrew month as the date of the onset of menses during the previous month, and during the same *onah*. For example, if she began her menses during the daytime hours of the 4th of *Tishrei*, the couple refrains from relations during the daytime hours of the 4th of *Cheshvan*.

The same interval: *veset haflagah*

This is the interval between the last two times that she began her period, counted from the date she last started her period. The day of onset of menses is counted twice: as the last day of the previous interval and as the first day of the new interval. For example, she began her menses on the 25th of *Tevet* and 26 days later on the 21st of *Shvat*. Counting the 21st of *Shvat* then again as day one of the next interval, her day of separation would be the 16th of *Adar*.[2]

The thirtieth day: *onah beinonit*

The "average" woman (the *beinonit*) is assumed to have an interval of thirty days, calculated as are the intervals described above. Thus all women who have not established a different pattern (as will be discussed below) halachically assume that they are like the average woman, and thus observe the thirtieth day from the time they first began to bleed as a time of separation. Because this day is based on "the general public" and not the individual woman, it has more stringent criteria. The *onah beinonit* always comes out four weeks and one day from the day she started bleeding.

Thus, a woman who has no established pattern has to anticipate her period on three dates: the Hebrew date, the interval and the thirtieth day. As half of the Hebrew months have 29 days, there is often an overlap and she actually only anticipates on two dates. On each *veset* she should do at least one internal exam to assure that she has not in fact begun her menses.

(For examples, see Part One, pp. 66–68, and Frequently Asked Questions at the end of this section, pp. 108–110.)

---

[2] Women who follow *Shulchan Aruch Harav* (Lubavitch) count the interval from the last day of bleeding, not the first.

An established pattern: *veset kavua*

If a woman establishes a pattern of commencing her menses on the same Hebrew date or after the same interval during the same *onah*, three cycles in a row, then she has as a *veset kavua* or established *veset*. This situation has two implications. There is a leniency involved, in that she needs to anticipate only the date or interval that she has established. There is also a stringency, in that a woman with a *veset kavua* MUST do an internal exam during that *onah*, or at least afterwards before the next time she has relations. By contrast, a woman who does not have a *veset kavua* should do an internal exam during the *onah*, but if she forgot she is not required to do one afterwards, except on the *onah beinonit*.

A woman who has a *veset kavua* separates each month only the *veset* she has established, unless she happens to see blood at a different date or interval. In that case, the following month (only) she has to keep the same Hebrew date and the interval (*chodesh* and *haflagah*) described above from the deviant sighting, in addition to her established date or interval.

If three cycles pass during which she does not begin her menses on her *veset kavua*, it is henceforth ignored. If she establishes a new *veset kavua*, then her previous one is permanently uprooted; otherwise, it is reinstated if she menstruates again, even once, in accordance with her former *veset kavua*.

In addition to three equal intervals or dates in a row, there are other ways of establishing a *veset kavua*. However, these are rare and rather complex. If a woman notices any pattern (menses on the same date every other month for example, or recurring variations in intervals) she should consult a rabbi.

Physical symptoms: *veset haguf*

A woman can also establish a *veset* based on certain physical symptoms. These symptoms have to be uniquely connected to her menses and to occur either immediately at the onset of menses or at a consistent interval beforehand. As the rules of *veset haguf* are complicated, women should note any premenstrual symptoms and when they occur in relation to the onset of menses. If she notices any pattern she should consult a rabbi.

Certain women are expected to be amenorrheic and do not have to anticipate getting their period. These include pregnant, nursing and postmenopausal women. Laws pertaining to each of these women are discussed in detail in the appropriate chapter in Part Three. The effect of hormonal contraception will be discussed in Part Four (pp. 167–168).

CHAPTER 4

BEHAVIOR WHILE *NIDDAH*

The serious punishment of *karet* applies to sexual intercourse during the *niddah* state. There is also a biblical prohibition to have any form of intimate physical contact such as hugging and kissing. By rabbinic decree, any contact such as touching or holding hands is forbidden as well.

A husband and wife may be alone unchaperoned during the *niddah* period (except for newlyweds who have not yet had marital relations for the first time). On the other hand, as the couple have a certain level of familiarity, there are additional prohibitions when she is a *niddah* to prevent situations and stimulation that could lead to forbidden intimacy. These prohibitions are known as *harchakot*. They can be grouped into a number of categories:

Further avoidance of touching
Passing objects from hand to hand is forbidden. Ashkenazic custom also prohibits sharing a seat if it moves (such as a swing), or if the weight of one person can be sensed by the other (e.g., a soft couch), unless there is a person or object between them.

Eating together
Certain rules apply to eating together:

> 1. A couple should not eat at the same table without a reminder that the wife is a *niddah*. This can be a private signal between the couple that is not obvious to others dining

with them. There are some opinions that this applies when they are eating alone, but not in the presence of other adults or children old enough to embarrass them.

2. A couple should not eat from the same plate.

3. The husband should not eat his wife's leftovers.

4. The husband should not drink his wife's leftover drink from the same cup, but the wife may drink after her husband.

Sharing a bed

While the wife is a *niddah,* the couple may not sleep in the same bed even if they are clothed, in different blankets, and not touching. Most couples have two different beds separated by a space, which can be moved together when relations are permitted.

The husband should not sit on his wife's bed in her presence. He may sit on the bed when she is not present, but not lie down there. The wife may sit on her husband's bed in his presence but not lie down. If he is absent, she may sit or lie on his bed.

Dress

The husband should not gaze at the parts of his wife's body that are generally covered. Gazing at parts that are uncovered such as her face is permitted, even if this gives him pleasure.

At the time when it was important for everyone to know if a woman was a *niddah* due to its effect on ritual purity, women wore special clothes while *niddah*. While this is no longer required, some continue the practice in a quiet way as another reminder to each other of their current status. The wife should not go out of her way to be enticing. However, as the halacha certainly does not want the couple to be turned off to each other, she can continue to dress to be attractive.

Signs of affection

There are three services that a wife normally performs for her husband that are considered to have specific overtones of affection and intimacy. Therefore, they may not be done in his presence in the normal fashion when she is a *niddah*. These are pouring wine, making a bed and drawing a bath.

Frivolous behavior

Frivolous and flirting behavior is prohibited. This does not preclude being friendly and considerate. Gestures such as letters, cards, small gifts, or flowers for Shabbat can help counterbalance the potentially lonely feeling of being a *niddah*.

When one of the couple is ill

If one of the couple is ill, and there is no one else to assist them, the spouse can provide whatever care is needed. The wife should be careful, however, not to do those things that particularly suggest intimacy. The rules are more stringent when the wife rather than the husband is ill. When she is ill, he should be particularly careful not to touch her, if possible. However, dealing with a dangerous illness takes precedence.

CHAPTER 5

FREQUENTLY ASKED QUESTIONS

1. I saw a bit of red on toilet paper and none on my underwear. What do I do?

This situation is a matter of debate. On the one hand, toilet paper is not susceptible to ritual impurity, and thus a stain would be permitted. This is particularly true if it she wiped the entire genital-rectal area and not just the vaginal outlet.[1] On the other hand, some authorities feel that a stain that comes from wiping the genital area cannot be treated with the leniencies of a stain on clothing, as it is obviously from her body,[2] among other considerations.[3] Therefore a woman should consult with her rabbi as to what to do in this situation. She should NOT do an internal *bedikah* as this will not help her and a problematic color on a *bedikah* cloth is likely to make her *niddah*.

It is important to point out that this is a situation that can be avoided. There is no obligation to examine the toilet paper.[4] If one cannot avoid doing so, one should wait at least 10 seconds before wiping to avoid the stringencies that accompany stains found immediately after urination. Also, there is no need for white toilet paper, even during the seven blood-free days. Therefore, women who feel the need to look (such as wanting to know if they are spotting during pregnancy) should consider using colored toilet paper, which will minimize the implications of finding stains.

---

[1] *Igrot Moshe*, YD 4:17[16].

[2] *Shulchan Aruch Harav*, comment on the end of YD 183.

[3] *Badei Hashulchan* 190:107.

[4] *Igrot Moshe*, YD 4:17[28]. Also see *Shiurei Shevet Halevi*, 191:20.

2. Does a small spot on a sanitary napkin make me *niddah?*

The status of stains on sanitary napkins is a matter of debate. On the one hand, many are made of absorbent cotton, which is not susceptible to ritual impurity, covered by paper or synthetic material. Others are made completely from synthetic material, which is not susceptible to ritual impurity. Therefore, it would seem that stains on sanitary napkins, in the absence of a halachically relevant sensation, would not make a woman *niddah.* There are, however, those who feel that since the napkins are made as a "garment," they can acquire ritual impurity and thus a stain on them does render a woman *niddah.* A woman should check with her rabbi as to his opinion, and act accordingly. If the rabbi indicates that a woman has to consider a stain on a napkin as a problem, but she feels more comfortable wearing something to absorb natural secretions, black panty liners may be a good solution.[5] As of this writing, there are several brands of black disposable panty liners available, as well as reusable colored cloth panty liners.

A woman should also ask the rabbi whether she is permitted to wear a napkin or panty liner during the seven clean days. In general, if stains on them are not considered to render her *niddah,* then she should not wear them during the seven blood free days, unless otherwise instructed.

3. What about tampons?

Tampons are inserted directly into the vaginal canal. Therefore, blood found on a tampon is similar to that found after an internal exam with a cloth (*bedikah*) or after intercourse, which would make a woman *niddah* even in the absence of *hargashah.* Therefore, although they are made of synthetic material, even a small spot on a tampon renders a woman *niddah.* It is therefore best to wear tampons only at times when one is already a *niddah.*

---

[5] Black panty liners are available in large Jewish communities and can be purchased online at www.mikvah.org.

4. How can I wear colored garments? Aren't I just ignoring something that is there?

When the rabbis enacted the decree that gave women the status of *niddah* even without "sensation," they included certain caveats. Thus, the same rabbis that enacted the stringency declared the leniency, and one need not hesitate to use it. The Rambam even states that the rabbis decreed that she *should* wear colored garments (when not in the seven blood-free days) to prevent her unnecessarily being prohibited due to stains.

5. I don't know how to swim and am afraid of the water. How can I go to the *mikveh*?

One does not need to be able to swim, as one is standing in chest-to shoulder-high water and only needs to immerse the rest of the body for a few seconds. If a woman is still scared, arrangements can be made for someone to enter the *mikveh* with her to support her. Any such fears should be discussed with the *mikveh* attendant. *Mikveh* attendants are usually willing to make accommodations for all sorts of extenuating circumstances.

6. The wife spends so much time preparing for the *mikveh*. What is the husband's role?

The halacha does not outline specific preparation for the husband for *mikveh* night. However, some women feel that if they have spent so much time in preparation, they would like their husband to also do "something." The "something" can be worked out between the couple. The following are suggestions that often arise:

1. A wife coming back "super clean" after preparation and immersion, will generally be happy to find that her husband has showered and, if relevant, shaved.

2. Some women like to have their husbands drive them to the *mikveh*. If so, for reasons of modesty, care should be taken that the husband parks in a place where he will not be seen and identified nor see and identify other women using the *mikveh*.

3. When the couple has children, the husband can play a key role in helping arrange child care so she can go to the *mikveh* at a convenient time. If he gets them to sleep before she comes back home, his wife will most likely greatly appreciate this.

4. Any small gesture that conveys the message – "I missed you, welcome back."

7. I have to go to the *mikveh* the night that we are invited to a wedding. What do I do?

First of all, one should see if one can use the *mikveh* before or after the wedding. In general, although *mikvaot* have posted hours, arrangements can be made in advance to go at different hours (sometimes an additional fee is charged for this service). If this is impossible, many excuses can be found to disappear for a short while from a crowd (I have to check on the children, I am going to visit a friend in the neighborhood who is sick). Untruths are permitted in these circumstances. Helpful hint: dry one's hair or make sure the wet hair is hidden, before returning to the *simchah*.

8. I have to go to the *mikveh* on Friday night and we are spending the weekend at my in-laws' house. What do I do?

Step one is to come up with a creative excuse (and smart mothers-in-law don't question too carefully!). However, if this is impossible, it is not a reason to delay going to the *mikveh*. While, in general, one tries to keep the fact that one is going to the *mikveh* private, telling another person so as to enable one to go is permitted.

9. I am still confused about when to go to the *mikveh*. Can I have a few more examples?

(All calendars in this chapter should be read from right to left.)

Tevet

Sat	Fri	Thur	Wed	Tues	Mon	Sun
ב	א					
ט	ח	ז	ו	ה	ד	ג
טז	טו	יד	יג	יב	יא	י
כג #	כב	כא	כ	יט	יח	יז
	כט	כח	כז #	כו #	כה #	כד #

A woman awoke on Shabbat the 23rd of *Tevet* at 8:00 am (the day *onah*) and saw a large stain on her white underwear. She is a *niddah* from this point.[6] She continued to bleed each day marked with a #. On Wednesday the 27th of *Tevet* (day number five of bleeding) in the afternoon she did a *hefsek taharah* which was fine. She places a *moch dachuk* at sunset and leaves it in place until nightfall. Thursday the 28th of *Tevet* is the first day of the seven clean days, and Wednesday the 5th of *Shvat* is the seventh. Assuming all the exams were acceptable, she goes to the *mikveh* on Wednesday night.

Shvat

Sat	Fri	Thur	Wed	Tues	Mon	Sun
א						
ח	ז	ו	ה	ד	ג	ב
טו	יד	יג	יב	יא	י	ט
כב	כא	כ	יט	יח	יז	טז
כט	כח	כז #	כו #	כה #	כד	כג
						ל

In the next example, she bled for three days in the month of *Shvat*, starting on a Monday night at 10 pm. Since the Hebrew day begins at

---

[6] When unsure whether the bleeding started in the *onah* one saw it or the previous *onah* (such as waking from sleep) we go by the *onah* that she is sure she saw it — generally the later one.

sunset, this is already considered Tuesday and thus she has bled on the 25th, 26th and 27th of *Shvat*. Assuming she is Ashkenazi and has no extenuating circumstances, she cannot commence the seven clean days until the 30th of *Shvat* as five days need to have passed which will end on the 29th of *Shvat*. In general she will do the *hefsek taharah* in this circumstance on Shabbat the 29th of *Shvat* in the afternoon. If she will not be near water or there are other problems, she can do it as early as Thurday the 27th when the bleeding stopped. In either case, however, the first of the seven clean days will be Sunday the 30th of *Shvat* and the last will be Shabbat the sixth of *Adar*. Assuming all *bedikot* are acceptable, she goes to the *mikveh* Saturday night.

Adar

Sat	Fri	Thur	Wed	Tues	Mon	Sun
ו	ה	ד	ג	ב	א	
יג	יב	יא	י	ט	ח	ז
כ	יט	יח	יז	טז	טו	יד
כז	כו #	כה #	כד #	כג #	כב #	כא #
					כט	כח

Nisan

Sat	Fri	Thur	Wed	Tues	Mon	Sun
ה	ד	ג	ב	א		
יב	יא	י	ט	ח	ז	ו
יט	יח	יז	טז	טו	יד	יג
כו	כה	כד	כג	כב	כא	כ
			ל	כט	כח	כז

She started bleeding on Sunday morning the 21st of *Adar*. She bled for six days and had a valid *hefsek taharah* on Friday afternoon the 26th of Adar. She placed a *moch dachuk*, which was fine, as was the *bedikah* of Shabbat the 27th. On Sunday, the 28th of *Adar* she had a large bright red stain on the her white underwear. In this case she has to begin the seven clean days again.

Since five days have already passed from the onset of *niddah*, she does not have to wait an additional five days.[7] An attempt at a *hefsek* on Sunday still has blood on it. She did a *hefsek taharah* and *moch* on Monday the 29th of *Adar* in the afternoon which were OK. The exams were OK from Tuesday the 1st of *Nisan* through Monday the 7th of *Nisan*. She goes to the *mikveh* that Monday night.

10. I am still confused about days of anticipation. Can I have a few more examples?

Tevet

Sat	Fri	Thur	Wed	Tues	Mon	Sun
ב #	א #					
ט	ח	ז	ו	ה #	ד #	ג #
טז	טו	יד	יג	יב	יא	י
כג	כב	כא	כ	יט	יח	יז
	כט	כח	כז (i)	כו	כה	כד

On each day marked with a # she bled, starting on the first of *Tevet* at 8:00 am (the day *onah*). This was the 27th day after the commencement of her menses the previous month. Her *onot prishah* for the following month are from sunrise to sunset on each of the following days:

    1. The first of *Shvat* (the Hebrew date) (d)

    2. The 27th of *Tevet* which is the 27th day (the interval) (i)

    3. The first of *Shvat* as it is also the 30th day (*onah beinonit*) (b)

Notice that her three times of separation "collapse" into two.

---

[7] As she was halachically forbidden to have relations, we are not concerned about *poletet shichvat zera* (see Part One, Chapter 3, pp. 45–46).

Shvat

Sat	Fri	Thur	Wed	Tues	Mon	Sun
א (b) (d)						
ח	ז	ו #	ה #	ד #	ג	ב
טו	יד	יג	יב	יא	י	ט
כב	כא	כ	יט	יח	יז	טז
כט	כח	כז	כו	כה	כד	כג
						ל

She in fact started bleeding on the Monday night after the 3rd of *Shvat*. This means the night *onah* of the 4th of *Shvat* as the Hebrew day starts the night before. The new interval is 33 days. Therefore the times of separation the following month are between sunset and sunrise on the following days:

1. The 4th of *Adar* (Hebrew date) (d)

2. The 6th of *Adar* (the interval – 33 days in this case)[8] (i)

3. The 3rd of *Adar*, which is the 30th day (*onah beinonit*) (b).

Adar

Sat	Fri	Thur	Wed	Tue	Mon	Sun
(i) ו	ה	(d) ד #	(b) ג #	ב #	א #	
יג	יב	יא	י	ט	ח	ו #
כ	יט	יח	יז	טז	טו	יד
כז	כו	כה	כד	כג	כב	כא
					כט	כח

---

[8] Notice this was arrived at by counting the first day of bleeding both as the last day of the previous interval and the first day of the new interval.

She in fact started bleeding on the morning of the first of *Adar*. During all her days of anticipation she is a *niddah* anyway so they have no practical significance. Her days for *Nisan* are:

1. The first of *Nisan* (the Hebrew date)

2. The 28th of Adar (the interval – 28 days in this case)

3. The 1st of Nissan (*the onah beinonit*)

Notice that although she has twice started bleeding on the first of the Hebrew month, this does not begin a pattern as they were interrupted by seeing on a different date in between.

11. I actually started bleeding before any days of anticipation, now what?

According to most opinions, for a woman who does not have a *veset kavua* for an interval (in other words most women) once one has started to bleed at a different interval the previous one is no longer valid and she can forget about it. The new interval day of anticipation is between her last menstrual period and the day that she just started. Similarly the *onah beinonit*, the 30th day, is now calculated from this new episode of bleeding. If she is earlier than usual by a few days her *onot prishah* come out during the time that she is a *niddah* and thus have little practical consequence. Should she start bleeding much earlier than anticipated, and stop bleeding by the time of the same Hebrew date, she does have to observe the Hebrew date as a day of anticipation with its attendant prohibition of intercourse. Should this come out to be her *mikveh* night, she should consult with a rabbi as to what to do.

12. It is three months since I had a baby and I have not yet been able to complete seven clean days and go to the *mikveh*. Help!

First it is important to realize that post partum bleeding (lochia) does last for a number of weeks (the average is 4 with about 10% of women having more than 6). Second, it is not unusual for postpartum bleeding to stop and then restart again – see section on childbirth in Part Three (p. 128) for more information. This is a time when the vaginal lining is more likely to be easily irritated due to the relatively low levels of estrogen at this time. One should definitely consult with a rabbi in this situation to see if the *moch* can be omitted temporarily and if the number of *bedikot* can be reduced. Once one has gone to the *mikveh*, this is a time of life when colored undergarments are highly recommended. When one is asking a rabbi questions about any stains that one sees, one should be sure to mention the amount of time that has gone by. If these halachic suggestions do not solve the problem, a physician should be consulted to see if temporary hormonal manipulation might help. If the problem is heavy bleeding rather than light spotting, then a physician should be consulted sooner to assure that there is nothing abnormal.

13. I am in my forties and having midcycle staining regularly, a day or so after *mikveh*. Is there anything I can do?

For women in their mid-forties who are in the time of life prior to menopause known as peri-menopause, this is a common situation. In order to deal with this issue, it is important to understand the halachic difference between "seeing blood," or bleeding, and finding a stain (*ketem*). What differentiates the two conditions is whether you had *hargashah*. If you did not have *hargashah*, the staining is considered a *ketem* and makes you *niddah* only if it meets certain conditions. It is NOT a problem if it is smaller than a certain size (a *gris*, approximately equivalent to the size of a US penny or Israeli shekel, see figure on page 33 above), is found on a colored surface, or is found on a surface that cannot obtain the status of ritual impurity. It should be noted that these leniencies DO NOT apply to stains found on an internal exam such as that done with a *bedikah* cloth. They also may not apply to stains found on toilet paper if you wiped deeply in the vaginal area or if you wiped in the vaginal area immediately after urinating.

In the question you posed, if you do not have *hargashah* and are referring to a *ketem*, and you are talking about a relatively small amount of bleeding, the situation can often be handled halachically. One such halachic solution is wearing colored underwear. While there is an opinion that clothing close to the body has to be evaluated more stringently, many authorities feel that stains on colored underwear would not make one *niddah*. Another potential halachic solution is pantyliners. Some authorities feel that these are a surface that cannot obtain the status of ritual impurity. As there is disagreement about this, you should ask a question of your rabbi prior to embarking on this method. The colored pantyliners that now exist have the advantage of combining two possible solutions. In addition, there is no halachic requirement to look at toilet paper, and you should avoid doing so.

If your staining is actually bleeding, then hormonal manipulation can often be used to help. In that case, please consult with a gynecologist. It is important that the physician understand that this bleeding is causing difficulties for you, as from a purely medical point of view it is generally not regarded as a problem and you may be told that it is simply a fact of life. If your physician would like further information about the laws of *niddah* or ways in which you can be helped, you may wish to refer him or her to www.JewishWomensHealth.org.

Note to the reader: Thousands of additional questions and answers can be found at Nishmat's Women's Health and Halacha website (www.yoatzot.org).

PART THREE

THE LIFE CYCLE

CHAPTER 1

PUBERTY

Age of onset of *niddah* status

תַּנְיָא: "אִשָּׁה" – אֵין לִי אֶלָּא אִשָּׁה – תִּינוֹקֶת בַּת יוֹם אֶחָד לְנִדָּה מִנַּיִן?
תַּלְמוּד לוֹמַר: "וְאִשָּׁה". (תלמוד בבלי; נדה לב.)

A woman can become a *niddah* at any age that she experiences uterine bleeding. This can even be soon after birth, when some female infants have bloody vaginal discharge due to withdrawal of the maternal hormones to which they were exposed in utero. She certainly becomes a *niddah* at the onset of menarche, and remains as such until she immerses in the *mikveh*, one of several reasons why physical contact between men and women is forbidden outside of marriage. Women do not enter a new status of being forbidden due to *niddah* upon marriage; rather, by immersing in the *mikveh* upon marriage they enter a new status of being permitted,[1] to their husbands. As the implications of being a *niddah* today primarily concern marital relations, the onset of regular menses has few halachic implications for unmarried girls.

Adolescence as a preparatory period

Adolescence, however, is a good time for a girl to begin to prepare by familiarizing herself with her body, its functions and its cycles. Girls can be taught to keep menstrual calendars from the beginning of menarche, which heightens their awareness of their cycles. This awareness can help in determining how to schedule their weddings when the time comes. From a

---

[1] As pointed out by a colleague Aliza Segal.

medical point of view it is also useful information in determining if there are any menstrual abnormalities. It is quite normal for menses to be irregular, even skipping quite a number of months, for the first two years after their onset. After this time, if they are still irregular, a medical consultation should be sought. It should also be noted that there is a great deal of normal variation in the age of onset of puberty. This is influenced by many factors, including genetics. The generally accepted time for concern and, thus, evaluation, is if a girl shows no signs of puberty by age 14[2] or has no menses by 16.[3]

Adolescence might also be a good time to begin to be made aware of the existence of *hilchot niddah*. While the full details are irrelevant at this point, discussing the outline can help dispel many myths and unnecessary fears. By providing a framework for later learning, it reduces the stress of learning the *halachot* in the rush prior to the wedding.

Learning to use tampons while young is also a good practice for the eventual need to do internal exams. It familiarizes girls with their anatomy and decreases the reticence in touching that part of the body. The hymen generally has a hole in the center through which menstrual blood exits. This hole is generally large enough to insert a small tampon. While tampon use may sometimes stretch the hymen, this does not change a woman's halachic status of virginity. Tampons should never be left in for over 24 hours, to prevent the possibility of toxic shock syndrome.

---

[2] Couchman GM and Hammond CB. "Physiology of Reproduction" in Danforth's *Obstetrics and Gynecology* 8th edition (Phil.: Lippincott, 1998).

[3] Hammond CB and Riddick DH. "Menstruation and Disorders of Menstrual Function" in Danforth's *Obstetrics and Gynecology* 8th ed. (Phil.: Lippincott, 1998).

CHAPTER 2

MARRIAGE

Setting the wedding date

The wedding should be set for a date when the bride does not expect to be a *niddah*. While the marriage ceremony would be valid even if she were, the bride being *niddah* leads to a stressful situation in which the newlyweds cannot be left alone.[1] It also necessitates slight changes in the ceremony to take into consideration the rules of *harchakot*. These are done discreetly, with only the minimum number of participants aware of the situation.

For a woman who has a very regular cycle, setting the date is relatively easy. There needs to be enough time after her previous menses that, after the cessation of bleeding, she can count seven blood-free days and then immerse in the *mikveh*. If her cycle is not predictable enough, or if there are unexpected changes, hormones can be used to prevent her being *niddah* at the time of her wedding.[2]

---

[1] In general, a husband is allowed to be alone (*yichud*) with his wife who is a *niddah*. Since the separation is temporary, we trust the couple to withstand temptation. This is not, however, the case when the couple has never yet had marital relations.

[2] There are also those who advocate use of hormones even for those women with a regular cycle due to the concern that the excitement of the wedding can lead to an irregular cycle. It should be remembered, however, that these are drugs with rare, but serious, side effects and thus a careful medical history needs to be taken prior to their use. Furthermore, sometime there is breakthrough bleeding from the use of the pills themselves, particularly in the first month of use. Thus weighing the risks and benefits of use versus non-use is an individual decision that should be made by the bride in consultation with her physician. For further discussion

There are two basic hormonal approaches. One is to use one of the many formulations of hormonal contraceptives. This is best done for a few cycles prior to the wedding, so that if there is any breakthrough bleeding from the hormones it can be controlled before the wedding. Another approach is to give progesterone to hold off the bleeding for a few days. The common drugs used are norethisterone acetate (Primolut-Nor) or medroxyprogesterone acetate (Aragest, Provera). Progesterone helps maintain the uterine lining. Thus giving supplementary progesterone starting about 5 days prior to the anticipated date of the next period will most likely succeed in delaying the onset of menses. Use for longer than about 10 days raises the chances of breakthrough bleeding. All of these are prescription drugs that should be used only under the supervision of a physician familiar with their use and who understands the implications of *hilchot niddah*. Not only does the bride not want her menses at her wedding, but all bleeding, including spotting, must stop at least 7 days prior to the wedding.

With the best of planning however, problems sometimes arise. It should be remembered in these circumstances, that marriage is meant to be forever and a few difficult weeks in the beginning should not overshadow a lifetime of happiness.

Immersion prior to the wedding

יָתֵר עַל זֶה: כָּל בַּת שֶׁתִּבְעוֹהָ לְהִנָּשֵׂא וְרָצְתָה – שׁוֹהָה שִׁבְעַת יָמִים נְקִיִּים מֵאַחַר שֶׁרָצְתָה, וְאַחַר כָּךְ תִּהְיֶה מוּתֶּרֶת לְהִבָּעֵל, שֶׁמָּא מֵחֲמוּדָהּ לָאִישׁ רָאֲתָה דָם טִיפָּה אַחַת וְלֹא הִרְגִּישָׁה בָּהּ. בֵּין שֶׁהָיְתָה הָאִשָּׁה גְדוֹלָה בֵּין שֶׁהָיְתָה קְטַנָּה, צְרִיכָה לֵישֵׁב שִׁבְעָה נְקִיִּים מֵאַחַר שֶׁרָצְתָה, וְאַחַר כָּךְ תִּטְבּוֹל וְתִבָּעֵל.
(רמב"ם; הלכות איסורי ביאה, יא: ט)

By rabbinical decree, a woman subsequent to a proposal of marriage has to consider herself a *niddah* even if she experienced no menstrual bleeding. Due to this halachic concern that minute bleeding might result from the anticipation (*dam chimud*), all women must count seven clean days and immerse in the *mikveh* prior to their wedding. If this is a first marriage,

---

see Zimmerman, DR. *Hormonal Intervention for the Prevention of Chuppat Niddah.* JME 2007; 6:11–14.

then she would have to do so anyway, as she remains a *niddah* until immersion even if years have passed since her last menses. However, even in the case of a second marriage where she had immersed in the *mikveh* after her last menses and had no further bleeding since, she still has to count seven days and immerse due to this decree.[3] Brides should try to go to the *mikveh* the day of the wedding or the previous evening. If circumstances dictate that this is difficult, she should consult with a rabbi as to the procedure to follow if immersing earlier.

The wedding ceremony[4]

The Jewish marriage procedure consists of two parts – *eirusin* or *kidushin* (betrothal[5]), and *nisu'in* (marriage). At one time these phases were separated by a number of months,[6] but today they are performed at the same time.[7]

By biblical law the *kidushin* requires three components:

---

[3] See Bleich JD. *Contemporary Halachic Problems III* (New York: Ktav, 1989) pp. 122–125 for debate on a bride who has no uterus.

[4] For further description of the Jewish marriage ceremony see:

Lamm M, *The Jewish Way in Love and Marriage* (San Francisco: Harper & Row, 1980) or

Kaplan A, *Made in Heaven* (New York: Moznaim, 1983)

[5] Although in modern Hebrew this is translated as engagement, in halachic usage it is the same as *kidushin. Eirusin/kidushin* makes a woman married to the extent that she would need a *get* (bill of divorce) to get out of this status, despite the fact that she is still not yet permitted to have relations with her husband. The term "engagement" is closer to *"shiduchin,"* which is declaring the intention to get married in the future. While breaking an engagement is unpleasant, it normally does not require a *get*.

[6] Generally, they waited 12 months for a first marriage and three months for a second marriage.

[7] *Tur, Even HaEzer* (EH) 62

והאידנא אין נוהגין ליארס אלא בשעת חופה.

A number of reasons have been given for the change in custom:

a. The fear of leaving the bride in a state of limbo if her groom did not appear at the appointed time, a situation that was a major concern in the uncertainty of times of persecution.

b. The temptation for the couple to commence intimate relations prior to the *kidushin* due to their feeling of being already partially married.

1. an act of betrothal

2. the future husband stating, or it being otherwise clear, that this was for the purpose of *eirusin*

3. at least two valid witnesses.

The Mishna enumerates three possible acts of betrothal: intercourse for the purpose of *eirusin*, by written contract, or the groom giving the bride an item of monetary value for the purpose of *eirusin*.

Due to the inherent immodesty involved, rabbinic law proscribed intercourse as an act of betrothal. The current method of betrothal is with an object of monetary value represented by the ring. To insure that its value is not subject to disagreement, it is generally a plain gold band without any precious stones.

Rabbinic law also added other requirements to *eirusin*:

1. A blessing on the *eirusin*[8]

...אֲשֶׁר קִדְּשָׁנוּ בְּמִצְוֹתָיו וְצִוָּנוּ עַל הָעֲרָיוֹת וְאָסַר לָנוּ אֶת הָאֲרוּסוֹת וְהִתִּיר לָנוּ אֶת הַנְּשׂוּאוֹת לָנוּ עַל יְדֵי חוּפָּה וְקִדּוּשִׁין. בָּרוּךְ אַתָּה ד' מְקַדֵּשׁ עַמּוֹ יִשְׂרָאֵל עַל יְדֵי חוּפָּה וְקִדּוּשִׁין.

> "...who commanded us with His commandments and se-
> parated us from the forbidden relationships and forbid us
> betrothed women and permitted us those who are married
> to us by the appropriate ceremonies. Blessed art Thou who
> sanctifies Israel with *chupah* and *kidushin*."

This blessing is generally preceded by a blessing over a cup of wine.

---

[8] This text is based on Rambam *Hilchot Ishut* 3:24. The word לנו (to us) was added to clarify the original, that only those married to us and not to others are permitted.

2. That the ceremony be performed with a *minyan* to ensure that it is public knowledge.

3. That a rabbi officiate at the ceremony.

However, the *kidushin* is valid even without these three conditions.

Marriage (*nisu'in*) consists of the act of the husband bringing the wife into his household. This is symbolized by "*chupah*." There is disagreement among the Rishonim[9] exactly what *chupah* is. In the present ceremony we cover all the opinions – the bride comes out among a multitude of people; a canopy is placed over the heads of the bride and groom; at the end of the ceremony they go to a private place and eat together (*yichud*).

Another requirement of *nisu'in* is the *ketubah* or marriage contract. This document (translated in Appendix G, p. 213) spells out the obligation of a husband to his wife. This is a necessary component of their being allowed to live together. Should the document be lost, a new one must be written immediately. The *ketubah* is generally read at the ceremony between the *kidushin* and the *nisu'in* to provide a separation between them.

Nisu'in must also take place in the presence of a *minyan* and has its own six blessings known as *birchot chatanim* ("the blessings of grooms"). These blessings are also preceded by a blessing over a cup of wine, leading to a total of seven known as *sheva brachot* (seven blessings).[10]

שֶׁהַכֹּל בָּרָא לִכְבוֹדוֹ. ...

"...Who has created everything for His honor."

---

[9] *Shulchan Aruch* EH 55:1.

[10] For the following six days after a first marriage for either party, at any time the bride and groom eat in the presence of a *minyan* these same blessings are said at the end of the grace after meals (*birkat hamazon*). In that case the blessing over the wine is as the seventh rather than the first blessing. These celebrations are known as *sheva brachot* as well. When it is a second marriage for both, the full *sheva brachot* are usually said only at the wedding ceremony and meal.

‫...יוֹצֵר הָאָדָם.‬

"...Creator of mankind."

‫...אֲשֶׁר יָצַר אֶת הָאָדָם בְּצַלְמוֹ בְּצֶלֶם דְּמוּת תַּבְנִיתוֹ וְהִתְקִין לוֹ מִמֶּנּוּ בִּנְיַן עֲדֵי עַד. בָּרוּךְ אַתָּה ד' יוֹצֵר הָאָדָם.‬

"...Who created Man in His image, in the image of His form, and established from him an everlasting building... who creates Man."

‫שׂוֹשׂ תָּשִׂישׂ וְתָגֵל הָעֲקָרָה בְּקִבּוּץ בָּנֶיהָ לְתוֹכָהּ בְּשִׂמְחָה. בָּרוּךְ אַתָּה ד' מְשַׂמֵּחַ צִיּוֹן בְּבָנֶיהָ.‬

"May the barren woman rejoice and be merry in the ingathering of her children in happiness... who gladdens Zion with her children."

‫שַׂמֵּחַ תְּשַׂמַּח רֵעִים הָאֲהוּבִים כְּשַׂמֵּחֲךָ יְצִירְךָ בְּגַן עֵדֶן מִקֶּדֶם. בָּרוּךְ אַתָּה ד' מְשַׂמֵּחַ חָתָן וְכַלָּה.‬

"May the loving friends be as happy as you made your creations in Eden happy...who gladdens the groom and bride."

‫...אֲשֶׁר בָּרָא שָׂשׂוֹן וְשִׂמְחָה חָתָן וְכַלָּה גִּילָה רִנָּה דִּיצָה וְחֶדְוָה, אַהֲבָה וְאַחֲוָה שָׁלוֹם וְרֵעוּת. מְהֵרָה ד' אֱלֹקֵינוּ יִשָּׁמַע בְּעָרֵי יְהוּדָה וּבְחוּצוֹת יְרוּשָׁלַיִם קוֹל שָׂשׂוֹן וְקוֹל שִׂמְחָה קוֹל חָתָן וְקוֹל כַּלָּה קוֹל מִצְהֲלוֹת חֲתָנִים מֵחֻפָּתָם וּנְעָרִים מִמִּשְׁתֵּה נְגִינָתָם. בָּרוּךְ אַתָּה ד' מְשַׂמֵּחַ חָתָן עִם הַכַּלָּה.‬

"...Who created joy and happiness, groom and bride, merriment, song, delight, love, brotherly love and friendship. Speedily may it be heard in the cities of Judah and the streets of Jerusalem, the sound of joy, the sound of happiness, the sound of a groom, the sound of a bride, the sound of grooms from their weddings and young men from their celebrations... who gladdens the groom with the bride."

Many customs have developed concerning weddings. The couple should consult with the rabbi to discuss which ones will be followed.

Changes in the ceremony if the bride is *niddah*

If the bride is *niddah,* there are minor modifications to the ceremony to accommodate the *harchakot* of a *niddah*. They are done discreetly with as few people as possible aware that anything is amiss.

1. Putting the ring on her finger – As she is not yet his wife prior to receiving the ring, he can put the ring on her finger trying not to touch her.

2. Drinking from the wine – In most American weddings the cup is given to the mother or mother-in-law to pass to the bride at all weddings, and thus one is not aware of when the bride is a *niddah*.

3. *Yichud* – Although a husband and wife can be alone together when the wife is a *niddah*, this applies only after the first episode of intercourse. Thus, if she is *niddah* at the wedding, they go off with singing and dancing toward the *yichud* room but the witnesses assure that they are not left alone.

4. After the wedding, arrangements need to be made that the husband and wife are not alone together. The arrangements should be discussed with a rabbi.

Hymenal bleeding

הַכּוֹנֵס אֶת הַבְּתוּלָה, בּוֹעֵל בְּעִילַת מִצְוָה וְגוֹמֵר בִּיאָתוֹ וּפוֹרֵשׁ מִיָּד... וּצְרִיכָה שֶׁתִּפְסוֹק בְּטָהֳרָה וְתִבְדּוֹק כָּל שִׁבְעָה, וְלֹא תַּתְחִיל לִמְנוֹת עַד יוֹם חֲמִישִׁי לְשִׁימוּשָׁהּ. וְנוֹהֵג עִמָּהּ כְּכָל דִּינֵי נִדָּה לְעִנְיַן הַרְחָקָה. (שולחן ערוך ; יורה דעה, קצג : א)

Although bleeding that may accompany the stretching of the hymen the first time a woman has intercourse[11] is clearly NOT uterine bleeding, by rabbinic decree this woman has the status of *niddah*. A couple where the wife is a virgin completes the first act of intercourse after the wedding but then observes all the laws of *niddah*,[12] even if they do not see any blood.[13] Unlike other circumstances, however, according to all traditions she only has to wait four days before starting to count the seven blood-free days. Sometimes her regular menses will begin during this time period, leading to a long time period before she can immerse in the *mikveh*. During all this time they have to observe all the separations incumbent on a couple where the wife is a *niddah*. Therefore, it is best to have the wedding about a week to 10 days after she could go to the *mikveh* so she will get her menses soon after the wedding and thus have a shorter period of separation. On the other hand, on the night of the wedding the couple may be tired and not quite ready to have full relations. Therefore, leaving a cushion of a few days before the menses are due is a good idea.

Occasionally, there continues to be bleeding from the hymen at subsequent episodes of intercourse. This would lead to another period of separation, which can be quite frustrating to a new couple. One way to avoid repeat bleeding is to assure that there is adequate lubrication prior to intercourse. This can be assisted by the use of products such as KY Jelly, a water soluble substance sold in pharmacies. Should repeat bleeding occur despite this, the wife should consult with a health care provider to determine what is the cause. If there is a thick or impenetrable hymen then this can be dealt with surgically. In most cases, gentle stretching, either manually or with dilators, can solve the problem.

---

[11] In many women today, particularly those who participate in active sports or use tampons, there will in fact not be bleeding. This does not change their status as *betulot* (virgins) in any way.

[12] There is one difference when the wife is *niddah* only because of *dam betulim*, but has not yet begun her menses. In that situation, either spouse may sit or lie on the other's bed; however, they may NOT both be on the same bed at the same time. (For the halacha at all other times, see pp. 75–76 and 100.)

[13] If the couple is not sure whether full penetration has taken place and there was no bleeding they should consult with a rabbi as to how to proceed.

CHAPTER 3

PREGNANCY

Effect on times of anticipation

רַבִּי אֱלִיעֶזֶר אוֹמֵר אַרְבַּע נָשִׁים דַּיָּן שְׁעָתָן: בְּתוּלָה, מְעֻבֶּרֶת מֵנִיקָה וּזְקֵנָה.
(משנה ; נדה א:ג)

    There are four categories of women who are halachically not ex-pected to menstruate. The pregnant woman is one of them. In practice this means that she does not have to keep *onot prishah* in anticipation of the onset of menses. There is a difference of opinion regarding the stage of pregnancy at which this status takes effect. Most authorities maintain that it applies after three months[1] have passed from her last *mikveh* use.[2] Rav Moshe Feinstein writes, however, that she has this status from the time of a positive pregnancy test.[3] For women without a *veset kavua* (the vast majority of women), there is little practical difference between the two opinions; once she misses her first period she has no date to calculate *onot prishah* for the following month. The woman with a *veset kavua* keeps her *veset* for three months according to the first opinion, and until the pregnancy test is positive according to Rav Feinstein.

---

[1] There is debate if this is three calendar months or 90 days. Farkas Y, *Sefer Taharah Kehalachah* (Jerusalem: Toras Chaim, 5758) p. 652.

[2] If she knows the date of conception (e.g., artificial insemination), she calculates from date of conception.

[3] *Igrot Moshe* YD 3:52. This probably applies as long as the pregnancy test results are after the first missed period as is generally the case at present.

If a woman bleeds during pregnancy, even after 90 days, then she keeps at least some of the *onot prishah*.[4] With the first episode, she keeps the same Hebrew date the next month. If she bleeds twice, she keeps both the Hebrew date and the interval between the two episodes. She does not establish a new *veset kavua* during pregnancy (or the following 24 months[5]) even if she sees three times on the same date or interval.

The fact that a woman is *mesuleket damim* (literally "her bleeding is absent") is important in deciding if stains are problematic or not. Therefore, a woman should mention the fact that she is pregnant when she asks a question about a stain.

---

[4] She should also notify her health care provider.

[5] During the twenty four months following childbirth a woman has the status of *meneket* – a nursing woman who is also not expected to have regular menses. She has this status whether she is breastfeeding or not (see further discussion in chapter on breastfeeding, p. 134).

CHAPTER 4

CHILDBIRTH

Status of *yoledet*

יוֹלֶדֶת, אֲפִילוּ לֹא רָאֲתָה דָם, טְמֵאָה כְּנִדָּה – בֵּין יָלְדָה חַי, בֵּין יָלְדָה מֵת, וַאֲפִילוּ נֵפֶל.
(שולחן ערוך ; יורה דעה, קצד:א)

    A vaginal delivery renders a woman a *yoledet*, a status which in practice is identical to *niddah*. This is true for a live birth, and also for a stillbirth or a miscarriage. A woman would become a *yoledet* even in the very unlikely circumstance that she experienced no bleeding at all.

From when in labor does the *yoledet* status begin?

שֶׁאִי אֶפְשָׁר לִפְתִיחַת הַקֶּבֶר בְּלֹא דָם. (תלמוד בבלי ; נדה כא:)

"It is impossible that the uterus opened without blood."

    Due to this principle that if the uterus opened there must have been blood, whether we saw it or not, any time there is sufficient opening of the uterus the *halachot* of *niddah* apply even if there is no visible blood. From the point of labor that a woman cannot walk unaided, she is assumed to have this degree of uterine opening.[2] Being told that she has a few centimeters of cervical opening by the obstetrician during pregnancy does

---

[2] *Shiurei Shevet Halevi* 194:2(4). This definition appears to be supported by the mishna in *Ohalot* 7:4.

not make her a *yoledet*. Flow of amniotic fluid just prior to childbirth may render her a *niddah* as it may have been accompanied by blood.[3] Leakage of amniotic fluid in the absence of blood at other times in her pregnancy would not render her a *niddah*.[4] The release of the mucus plug ("the bloody show") is a matter of debate but many authorities maintain that this blood is not uterine in origin and would not render her a *niddah*.[5]

Cessation of the *yoledet* status

The procedure for exiting the *yoledet* status is the same as that for exiting *niddah*. One waits a minimum of five days from the onset of bleeding, performs a *hefsek taharah*, counts seven blood-free days, and immerses in the *mikveh*.

The bleeding that follows childbirth (lochia) generally continues for a number of weeks. The median duration is 28 days; however, two or even three months of bleeding is normal. It is also normal for bleeding to stop completely and then start again. Therefore, in practice, it may take a number of attempts over several months for a woman to get to the *mikveh* following childbirth.

During this process, it is especially important to ask halachic questions. Certain colors may be permissible, and a rabbi may instruct a woman to perform fewer *bedikot* or to omit the *moch dachuk* during the time her body is recovering from childbirth. If bleeding continues for more than eight weeks, she should have a gynecological exam to confirm that the bleeding is still uterine and not vaginal.

The *yoledet* status: biblical and rabbinic law

According to biblical law, a woman following childbirth could immerse in the *mikveh* on the night of the seventh day (i.e., the beginning of the eighth day) following the birth of a boy, or on the night of the fourteenth day (i.e., the beginning of the fifteenth day) following the birth of a girl, regardless of whether her bleeding had stopped.

---

[3] *Shiurei Shevet Halevi* 194:2(4).

[4] But it does mean that she should be checked immediately by a physician.

[5] Forst B, *The Laws of Niddah Vol I* (New York: Mesorah, 1997) p. 465.

וְכַמָּה הֵם יְמֵי טוּמְאָתָהּ? עַכְשָׁיו בַּזְמַן הַזֶה, כָּל הַיוֹלְדוֹת חֲשׁוּבוֹת יוֹלְדוֹת בְּזוֹב
וּצְרִיכוֹת לִסְפּוֹר שִׁבְעָה נְקִיִּים; נִמְצֵאתָ אוֹמֵר שֶׁיוֹלֶדֶת זָכָר יוֹשֶׁבֶת שִׁבְעָה לַלֵידָה
וְשִׁבְעָה נְקִיִּים לַזִיבָה, וְהַיוֹלֶדֶת נְקֵבָה יוֹשֶׁבֶת שְׁבוּעַיִם לַלֵידָה וְשִׁבְעָה נְקִיִּים לַזִיבָה.
יְמֵי לֵידָה – שֶׁהֵם שִׁבְעָה לְזָכָר וְאַרְבָּעָה עָשָׂר לִנְקֵבָה – אִם לֹא רָאֲתָה בָּהֶן, עוֹלִים
לִסְפִירַת זִיבָתָהּ; וְאִם שָׁלְמוּ שִׁבְעָה נְקִיִּים בְּתוֹךְ אַרְבָּעָה עָשָׂר לִנְקֵבָה, הֲרֵי זוֹ אֲסוּרָה
עַד לֵיל חֲמִישָׁה עָשָׂר; וְאִם טָבְלָה קוֹדֶם לְכֵן, לֹא עָלְתָה לָהּ טְבִילָה.
(שולחן ערוך; יורה דעה, קצד:א)

Today, however, all women are considered to have entered child-birth in a status of *zavah*, and thus must count seven blood-free days before going to the *mikveh*. These seven days can be counted as soon as all bleeding has ceased, assuming the five day minimum has passed. In the very unlikely event that a woman has minimal bleeding, she cannot immerse in the *mikveh* until twelve days after the birth of a boy or fourteen days after the birth of a girl. (If she was already *niddah* when she went into labor, counting the five day minimum from the onset of *niddah*, she could immerse as early as seven days after the birth of a boy.) As we have seen, in reality it is generally a much longer period, as bleeding generally continues for a number of weeks.

אֲבָל אִם חָזְרָה וְרָאֲתָה, אֲפִילוּ טִיפַּת דָם כְּחַרְדָּל, טְמֵאָה. אַף עַל גַּב דְּמִדְאוֹרַיְיתָא דָם
טָהוֹר הוּא, כְּבָר פָּשַׁט הַמִּנְהָג בְּכָל יִשְׂרָאֵל שֶׁאֵין בּוֹעֲלִין עַל דָם טָהוֹר, וְדִינוֹ כִּשְׁאָר דָם
לְכָל דָּבָר. (רמ"א, שולחן ערוך; יורה דעה, קצד:א)

By biblical law, before it became accepted that all women in child-birth have the status of *zavah*, and before the five-day minimum was enacted, a woman could immerse in the *mikveh* as soon as the seven-day (boy) or fourteen-day (girl) time frame had passed – even if she continued to bleed. Any bleeding in the following thirty-three days for a boy and sixty-six days for a girl was considered *dam tohar*, which rendered her unfit to bring sacrifices in the Temple, but did not forbid relations with her husband. By now, the custom has been accepted by all communities that any uterine bleeding during this period renders her a *niddah*.

Attendance of husband at delivery

As the rules of conduct with a *niddah* apply to a *yoledet*, there are halachic problems with a husband seeing his wife undressed at this time. Furthermore, there is an objection in the halacha for a husband to look directly at the vaginal opening of his wife, even when she is not a *niddah*. On the other hand, women in childbirth are both medically and halachically known to be assisted by emotional support during a process that, while producing wonderful results, is often painful and frightening. These factors need to be taken into consideration while the couple decides if the husband will attend the delivery.[6, 7, 8, 9]

If the husband does attend:

1. The couple should request that a mirror NOT be placed in front of the woman to allow direct visualization by the husband of the exiting child.

2. The couple should request that the wife be kept as covered as possible or that a screen be placed between her upper and lower body. (This is done routinely for cesarean deliveries and thus is not difficult to arrange.)

3. The husband should not touch his wife unless there is no one else to help her.

---

[6] Rav Moshe Feinstein (*Igrot Moshe* YD 2:75) states that attendence of the husband is permitted.

[7] *Bnei Banim* Volume 1 Number 33.

[8] Zohar N. *"Kurs Hachanah L'leidah." Techumin* 5757 17:198–201.

[9] Steinberg A, "Natural Childbirth: May the Husband Attend?" *Journal of Halacha and Contemporary Society* 1981; 1:107–122.

Cesarean section

יוֹצֵא דֹפֶן – אִם לֹא יָצָא דָם אֶלָּא דֶרֶךְ דֹפֶן, אִמּוֹ טְהוֹרָה מִלֵּידָה וּמִנִּדָּה וּמִזִּיבָה.
(שולחן ערוך ; יורה דעה, קצד: יד)

The rules of *yoledet* do not apply to birth by cesarean section. Thus, if a woman who underwent a cesarean had no bleeding via the vagina (an extraordinarily rare occurrence) she would be neither a *niddah*, *zavah*, or a *yoledet* and would not have to go to the *mikveh* after childbirth. In reality, most women who have a cesarean continue to have bleeding via the vagina from the uterus as they shed the remains of the uterine lining from pregnancy. Therefore the laws of *niddah* would apply to them. However, they can begin to count seven clean days as soon as the bleeding has ceased (after a minimum of 4 or 5 days) and do not have to wait 14 days before immersion if a girl was born.

Miscarriage

Spontaneous abortions or "miscarriages" are a very common occurrence, with about 15% of all clinically recognized pregnancies ending this way. The incidence increases with age, rising from 12% in women less than 20 years old to over 50% in women over 45 years of age. When a miscarriage happens in the first trimester it is generally due to an abnormality in the fetus.[10] A single miscarriage is generally not a cause for medical concern.[11] Habitual abortion (generally defined as 3 or more miscarriages) requires investigation. There are a number of categories relating to spontaneous abortions – threatened, inevitable, incomplete or missed. Bleeding from any of these, as it is from the uterus, would render a woman a *niddah* unless it fits into the category of permitted stains (see Part One, chapter 1, pp. 32–35).

---

[10] Scott JR. "Early Pregnancy Loss" in *Danforth Obstetrics and Gynecology* (8th edition) [ed Scott JR, Di Saia PJ, Hammond CB, Spellacy WN] Phil.: Wilkins, 1998.

[11] Emotionally, however, even one miscarriage is painful, particularly during a later trimester. The couple should be allowed to grieve their loss. Comments such as "you can always have more kids" or "it was all for the best" are not helpful.

הַמַּפֶּלֶת בְּתוֹךְ אַרְבָּעִים אֵינָהּ חוֹשֶׁשֶׁת לְוָלָד אֲבָל חוֹשֶׁשֶׁת מִשּׁוּם נִדָּה, אֲפִילוּ לֹא רָאֲתָה. (שולחן ערוך ; יורה דעה, קצד:ב)

מִפְּנֵי שֶׁאִי אֶפְשָׁר לִפְתִיחַת הַקֶּבֶר בְּלֹא דָם, וְנָפְקָא מִינַּהּ דְּמִיָּד לְאַחַר שֶׁסָּפְרָה שִׁבְעָה נְקִיִּים מוּתֶּרֶת וְאֵינָהּ חוֹשֶׁשֶׁת לְוָלָד. (רמא ; שם)

While the rules of *yoledet* apply after a miscarriage, this is only if it happens more than forty days after conception. These forty days are counted from the night of immersing in the *mikveh* and thus generally correlate with about seven and a half weeks of gestation as calculated medically.[12]

If the sex of the fetus is unknown (as is often the case in miscarriages), then we go by the more stringent situation of assuming it is a girl and a minimum of 14 days is needed before *mikveh* immersion. If it is known that the fetus is a boy and all bleeding has ceased by the end of day five, then she could immerse the night after day 12 (after completion of the *shiva neki'im*). Generally, however, bleeding lasts longer than a week, so the distinction is rarely practical.

---

[12] Obstetricians calculate weeks of gestation from the last menstrual period, even though this leads to the anomalous situation that a woman is almost two weeks pregnant at the time that she conceives. *Mikveh* night is generally at least 12 days after the onset of the last menstrual period. Twelve plus 40 is 52, which is 7.5 weeks according to this medical counting.

CHAPTER 5

BREASTFEEDING

Medical background

Breastfeeding is endorsed by major health organizations as the optimal form of infant nutrition. It also has multiple health benefits for both the mother and infant. To quote the 1997 policy statement of the American Academy of Pediatrics[1]

> Human milk is uniquely superior for infant feeding and is species-specific; all substitute feeding options differ markedly from it... Epidemiologic research shows that human milk and breastfeeding of infants provide advantages with regard to general health, growth and development, while significantly decreasing risk for a large number of acute and chronic conditions. Research in the United States and Canada, Europe and other developed countries, among predominately middle class populations provide strong evidence that human milk feeding decreases the incidence and/or severity of diarrhea, lower respiratory infection....

> Exclusive breastfeeding is ideal nutrition and sufficient to support optimal growth and development for approximately the first 6 months after birth... Gradual intro-

---

[1] American Academy of Pediatrics, "Breastfeeding and the Use of Human Milk," *Pediatrics* 1997; 100:1035–1039. These points have been expanded in the 2005 policy statement, *Pediatrics* 2005; 115:496–506.

duction of iron enriched solid foods in the second half of the first year should complement the breast milk diet. It is recommended that breastfeeding continue for at least 12 months, and thereafter for as long as mutually desired…

From the halachic perspective of preserving one's health it is also optimal.

Effect on times of anticipation

מֵנִיקָה כָּל עֶשְׂרִים וְאַרְבַּע חוֹדֶשׁ אַחַר לֵידַת הַוָּלָד – אֵינָה קוֹבַעַת וֶסֶת. אֲפִילוּ מֵת הַוָּלָד אוֹ גְמָלַתּוּ, דָּמִים מְסֻלָּקִים מֵהֶן כָּל זְמַן עִיבּוּרָהּ וְכָל עֶשְׂרִים וְאַרְבַּע חוֹדֶשׁ. וּמִכָּל מָקוֹם, חוֹשֶׁשֶׁת לִרְאִיָּה שֶׁתִּרְאֶה, כְּדֶרֶךְ שֶׁחוֹשֶׁשֶׁת לְוֶסֶת שֶׁאֵינוֹ קָבוּעַ. (שלחן ערוך ; יורה דעה, קפט:לג)

Halachically speaking, a *meneket* is a woman within twenty-four months after birth, whether breastfeeding or not.[2] During this time she is considered *mesuleket damim*[3] and thus she does not have to anticipate her menses as long as she does not bleed.[4] Thus she does not observe *onot prishah* as long as she does not have any bleeding after the cessation of her postpartum bleeding.

If she does bleed, she observes the Hebrew date the following month. If she bleeds twice she begins to observe the Hebrew date and the interval. There is a difference of opinion as to whether she observes the *onah beinonit*.[5] During this period, however, she does not establish a *veset kavua* if her menses follow a regular pattern.

---

[2] *Shulchan Aruch* YD 189:33.

[3] Mishna *Niddah* 1:3

[4] For a discussion of the current length of lactational amenorrhea vs the talmudic assumptions, see Zimmerman DR. "Lactational Amenorrhea and *Mesuleket Damim* – a Medical-Halakhic Analysis." *B'or Hatorah* 2002; 13E:174–184.

[5] The *Sidrei Taharah* brought by the *Pitchei Teshuvah* YD 189:31 states that she does not and this is what Rav Mordechai Eliyahu states in his guidebook *Darchei Taharah*. Rav Moshe Feinstein feels that since most women nowadays are NOT amenorrheic for this long she should keep the thirtieth day.

Other *halachot* of breastfeeding

Breastfeeding for at least two years is halachically encouraged.[6] Breastfeeding directly from the breast is permitted until the fifth birthday unless the child stopped breastfeeding by his own volition for seventy-two hours after the end of the twenty-fourth month of life. Expressed breastmilk is permissible at any age.[7] Breastmilk is parve, although it should not be mixed directly with meat products as it appears too much like mixing meat and milk.

Breastfeeding is also a universally halachically accepted method of spacing children. While breastfeeding is not a foolproof method of birth control, in the first 6 months, if the mother has not yet resumed menses and the baby is exclusively breastfeeding, the rate of pregnancy is less than 1%. Further discussion will be found in the section on birth control (pp. 162–163).

---

[6] *Pitchei Teshuvah* YD 81:16.

[7] For further discussion of the halachic implications of breastfeeding see Zimmerman, Deena R, "Duration of Breastfeeding in Jewish Law" in Safrai, C and Halpern, M (eds.) *Jewish Legal Writings by Women* (Jerusalem: Urim Publications, 1997).

CHAPTER 6

THE CLIMACTERIC (MENOPAUSE, PERI-MENOPAUSE)

Medical background

A woman has the maximum number of ova (eggs) that she will have during her life when she is a fetus of about twenty weeks gestation. At this point, there are about 6–7 million oocytes (egg cells), which decrease to about 2 million by the time she is born. At puberty there are about 400,000. During the course of a woman's lifetime, the number of remaining ova decreases, with about 20,000 left in the late thirties. The menopause is that point in time when permanent cessation of menstruation occurs due to loss of ovarian activity and the depletion of follicles.

The period of time immediately before and after menopause is known as the peri-menopause. This is a transition that usually occurs between regular cycling and menopause, characterized by hormonal fluctuation roughly two to eight years before and one year after the last natural period.[1] The average age of menopause is 50 years ± 8 years. Women who undergo surgical removal of their ovaries at a younger age will experience menopause earlier.

Due to this process, toward the late thirties and early forties, women will start to notice that their cycle is changing.[2] Often the intervals between cycles become shorter, and thus they are in a *niddah* status more often. There can be more episodes of mid-cycle staining, and many women

---

[1] Nachtigall LE. "The Symptoms of Perimenopause." *Clinical Obstetrics and Gynecology* 1998; 41:921–927.

[2] Klein NA, Soules MR. "Endocrine Changes of the Perimenopause." *Clinical Obstetrics and Gynecology* 1998; 41:912–920.

start to experience brown discharge in the days before their menses actually begin. Thus many questions of *niddah* arise. While these changes are biologically normal, they can be halachically quite frustrating. Toward the late forties and early fifties, intervals between cycles get longer and are often irregular, a further sign of ensuing menopause. At some point, menses cease. Should bleeding resume at this time of life after one year of amenorrhea, a woman should be examined by a physician to rule out cancer.

Effect on times of anticipation

From a halachic point of view, the "elderly woman" is one of the four women who are considered to be *mesuleket damim*, and thus does not need to observe the *onot prishah*.[3]

אֵיזוֹ הִיא זְקֵנָה? כָּל שֶׁעָבְרוּ עָלֶיהָ שָׁלֹשׁ עוֹנוֹת סָמוּךְ לְזִקְנָתָהּ.
(משנה; נדה א:ה)

  The mishna explains that an elderly woman is one who has not had menses for 3 *"onot"* (later explained as 30 days each, for a total of 90 days[4]) at the time of "her elderliness." Regarding the age at which a woman is halachically considered "elderly," there are differences of opinion in the sources.[5] On a practical level, any woman who has not had any menses for ninety days no longer observes the times of separation. She does, however, observe all the laws of *niddah* if she actually bleeds.[6]

---

[3] Mishna *Niddah* 1:3

[4] *Niddah* 9b

[5] Steinberg A. *Encyclopedia Hilchaltit Refuit*. (Jerusalem: Machon Schlesinger, 1988) s.v. *zekenah*.

[6] By this point, the Hebrew date of her previous menses would have passed, as would the thirtieth day and her previous interval, unless that was also 90 days. Thus, it would be an extremely rare case of a woman who had a *veset kavua* of an interval of 90 days who would still need to keep the days of separation regardless of her age.

Hormone replacement therapy (HRT)

The lack of ovarian estrogen not only leads to cessation of menses but to other physiological changes. Early in the menopause many woman complain of vasomotor problems ("hot flashes"), psychogenic disturbances (mood changes, sleeping difficulty, memory loss) and uro-genital complaints such as vaginal dryness. In order to prevent these phenomena, regimens of hormonal replacement were devised which continue the administration of estrogen.

It should be noted that a number of recent studies have questioned the widespread use of HRT. A large study known as the Women's Health Initiative was stopped in July 2002 as the women taking a particular combination of estrogen and progesterone had increased risk of breast cancer and thrombotic diseases such as heart attacks, strokes and blood clots.[7, 8] Other studies have also raised concerns about increased breast cancer rates in women taking HRT.[9] A woman should carefully discuss the options with her health care provider. However, if, for her, the benefits outweigh the risks, the effects on *hilchot niddah* are as follows:

First of all, if a woman having cyclical bleeding due to hormonal contraception goes directly on to cyclical hormonal replacement therapy, she can continue to become a *niddah* monthly past even the advanced ages given for elderliness.

When to observe the *onot prishah* while on HRT evokes a debate similar to that involved in the use of birth control pills. One possibility is to ignore the fact that she is taking hormones and to observe the Hebrew date in the next month, the interval between the last two periods, and the

---

[7] Manson JE, Hsia J, Honson KC, Rossouw JE, Assaf AR, Lasser NL, Trevisan M, Black HR, Heckbert SR, Detrano R, Strickland OL, Wo ND, Crouse JR, Stein E, Cushman M; Women's Health Initiative Investigators. "Estrogen Plus Progestin and the Risk of Coronary Heart Disease." *NEJM* 2003; 349:523–34.

[8] Chlebowski RT, Hendrix SL, Langer RD, Stefanick ML, Gass M, La Rodabough RJ, Gilligan MA, Cyr MG, Thomson CA, Khendekar J, Petrovitch H, McTeirnan A; WHI Investigators. "Influence of Estrogen Plus Progestin on Breast Cancer and Mammography." *JAMA* 2002; 289:3243–53.

[9] Li CI, Malone KE, Porter PL, Weiss NS, Tang MT, Cushin-Haugen Daling JR. "Relationship Between Long Durations and Different Regiments of Hormone Therapy and Risk of Breast Cancer." *JAMA* 2003; 289:3254–63.

thirtieth day, as does any woman who has not established a *veset kavua*. Others, such as Rav Mordechai Eliyahu, view hormones as establishing their own type of *veset*, and thus if she regularly sees blood a specific number of days after stopping the medication that would be her *veset*. A rabbi should be consulted.

Thought should be given to the type of HRT chosen. Cyclic therapy will continue to give a monthly withdrawal bleed and thus monthly separation due to *niddah*. Continuous therapy is more likely to induce amenorrhea. However, this method is also most likely to induce irregular bleeding and spotting, as can unopposed estrogen.[10] Minor bleeding episodes can be generally managed halachically by the use of colored underwear and not looking.[11] Heavier bleeding may be more problematic. Change in the hormone dosage can sometimes change the frequency of bleeding problems.

For the prevention of osteoporosis only, other medical approaches exist. These include the use of selective estrogen receptor modulators such as raloxifene. Biphosphonates such as alendronate and risedronate are also used to help build up bone. None of these treatments affect the menstrual cycle and hence do not affect a woman's *niddah* status.

---

[10] Pickar JH, Bottiglioni F, Archer DF. "Amenorrhea Frequency with Continuous Combined Hormone Replacement Therapy: a Retrospective Analysis." *Climacteric* 1998; 1:130–6.

[11] This is because in the absence of *hargashah* this bleeding is considered a "stain" (*ketem*), not actual menstruation, and is forbidden by rabbinical and not biblical decree. The decree does not apply to stains on colored garments. As long as the stain is on a colored garment, unless it is used for an internal examination (*bedikah*), she does not have the status of *niddah* even, according to most *poskim*, if found on tight garments such as underwear. The exact details of how and when to do this should be discussed with a rabbi.

PART FOUR

MEDICAL ISSUES

CHAPTER 1

GENERAL DIAGNOSTIC EXAMINATIONS

Halachic background

Three issues are involved in determining whether a particular medical examination renders a woman *niddah*. First, if she bled during or after the examination, can we be reasonably sure that the bleeding is from the trauma of the exam, and not uterine bleeding that would render her a *niddah*? Second, even if she did not visibly bleed, nevertheless, was the uterus "opened" according to the Talmudic principle of "there is no opening of the uterus without blood"?[1] Third, at what point in her cycle did the bleeding occur?

Procedures carried out entirely within the vaginal canal would NOT make her a *niddah*. Thus, a simple, standard manual exam by a doctor does not change her status. Bleeding from such a procedure can be attributed to injury by the examination. When the bleeding results from a procedure inside the uterus, it is more difficult to be sure that the bleeding is only from trauma. Some rabbis are more lenient with this than others.[2] Concerning bleeding from the cervix, there is disagreement among the

---

[1] Actually there is an additional issue: whether we accept the testimony of the physician as to the source of the bleeding. However, Rav Moshe Feinstein (*Igrot Moshe* YD 4:17[17]) answers that all physicians can be relied upon to state what they see. Experts in the field (gynecologists, for example) can also be trusted to estimate if a lesion they saw can bleed, or that a particular procedure is likely to cause bleeding. This applies to all physicians regardless of religious background, as they are simply stating the facts of their profession.

[2] Forst B. *The Laws of Niddah Vol I* (New York: Mesorah, 1997) pp. 428–429.

authorities as to whether it should be judged like bleeding from the vagina or from the uterus. Most authorities rule that certainly bleeding from the OUTSIDE of the cervix is similar to that from the vagina.

Before scheduling any gynecological procedure, the doctor should be asked what is the likelihood of bleeding resulting from the procedure, does the instrument enter the cervix, and if so, what is the diameter of the instrument used, and whether the procedure needs to be done at a specific point in the monthly cycle. This information should be discussed with a rabbi to determine what effect the examination will have on the woman's *niddah* status.

Uterine Opening

The size of the instrument is important because even if there is no evident bleeding, a medical procedure can render a woman a *niddah*.[3] The Talmud in *Niddah* 21b records a dispute as to whether the womb can open without the expulsion of any blood, even if no blood is seen. The Shulchan Aruch[4] and all later authorities accept the view that the uterus cannot open without blood. However, the later authorities disagree as to whether this relates only to the spontaneous natural opening of childbirth ("from the inside") or includes interventional opening ("from the outside").[5] There is a further disagreement as to whether the latter refers to the opening of the internal[6] or of the external opening of the cervix or "os."[7]

There is, however, a minimum size of the opening that would make her a *niddah*. Rav Moshe Feinstein states this is greater than 19 mm (3/4 inch).[8] *Badei Hashulchan* brings a measurement of 15 mm.[9] As the natural

---

[3] For further discussion of this topic see:

1) Pris Y. *"Hetken Toch Rechmi VeTzilume Rechem."* *Techumin* 5755; 15:328–47.

2) Brander K. "Gynecological Procedures and Their Interface with Halacha." *Journal of Halacha and Contemporary Society* 2001; 42:31–45.

[4] *Shulchan Aruch* YD 194:2, 188:3, 6.

[5] *Noda beYehuda Mahadura Tinyana*, YD 120.

[6] *Igrot Moshe* YD 1:83, *Orach Chaim* 3:100.

[7] *Shiurei Shevet Halevi* 188:3[4].

[8] *Igrot Moshe* YD 1:89.

[9] *Badei Hashulchan* YD 194:31.

opening of the uterus, except during childbirth, is approximately 3 mm, to put an instrument as large as these into the uterine opening would require sedation; thus most office procedures should NOT make a woman a *niddah* due to uterine opening.[10] It is important to ask the doctor the diameter of the instrument that he inserted and whether he noticed any bleeding from the uterus prior to the procedure, and pass on this information to the rabbi.

Timing of medical examinations

From the time a woman goes to the *mikveh* until her days of anticipated menses, she has a halachic presumption that she is not *niddah* (*chezkat taharah*). Therefore, it is easier for bleeding during this time frame to be considered as of traumatic origin. It is usually best that gynecological exams not be scheduled during the seven blood-free days,[11] as during this time we are trying to establish the absence of uterine bleeding, and the rulings are more strict. Similarly, it is best not to schedule an exam on a day of anticipated menses. However, if the exam indeed must be done at that time, she should consult a rabbi, without assuming on her own that she has to begin counting again or that her menses began. If the exam itself will make her *niddah*, the woman might prefer to have it done close to the time that she is *niddah* anyway. It is a good idea to wear colored underwear (except during the blood-free days) and to avoid looking at toilet paper after an exam, in case of light spotting.

Specific examinations

Manual exam

This exam consists of the physician inserting one or two gloved fingers into the vagina. This is often done during pregnancy to determine the degree of opening of the cervix. Sometimes the other hand palpates (feels) the abdomen, in which case it is known as a bimanual exam. This exam is done totally within the vaginal canal and nothing enters the uterus. There is generally no bleeding with this exam. A small amount of blood on the gloved fingers can be attributed to abrasion (scratching) of the walls of the

---

[10] *Nishmat Avraham* YD 194.

[11] Especially the first three days when the rulings are stricter.

vagina, especially if the woman is in a condition where her vaginal lining is friable (likely to bleed with minimal cause) such as pregnancy, certain parts of the menstrual cycle, after menopause, or while taking hormonal contraceptives. Thus in most cases a bimanual exam does not render a woman a *niddah*.

Speculum examination

In this exam, a metal (or plastic) instrument consisting of two rounded blades on a hinge is placed in the vaginal canal and then the blades are opened. This allows direct visualization of the mouth (os) of the cervix, the opening of the uterus. The speculum does not enter the cervical canal at all, and this exam should not present a problem of *niddah* due to opening of the uterus.[12] The doctor can report that he sees no blood exiting the cervix; only if blood is seen exiting the cervix does the woman become a *niddah*. There is generally no bleeding at all with this exam, or else a small amount of blood on the blades of the speculum can be attributed to abrasion of the walls of the vagina. This is especially true if the woman is in a condition where her vaginal lining is friable and when lubrication was not used.[13]

Papanicolaou (Pap) smear

This exam is done as a screening test for cervical cancer.[14] Performing a Pap smear includes a speculum examination, as the speculum is used to

---

[12] There is an opinion (Rav Mordechai Eliyahu in *Darchei Taharah*) that the blades, if separated more than 5 cm, can open the external os sufficiently to cause *"petichat hakever"* for those who maintain that the external os is the subject of discussion. Most *poskim* rule differently.

[13] Gynecological exams are often done with lubricating jelly. However, when a pap smear is done only water is used, as the jelly can interfere with histology results.

[14] This cancer is most common in younger women. When detected early it is completely curable, and thus screening with a Pap smear is highly recommended. The US recommendation is for an annual exam, although other countries recommend it every two years after repeated negative exams. While cervical cancer is less likely with monogamous women (as one of its causes is infection with the sexually transmitted disease papilloma virus or venereal warts) it can occur, and should be screened for. This screening is recommended even for women who have been vaccinated against this virus. Women should discuss this vaccine with their health care provider.

visualize the opening of the cervix. The smear consists of a few cells that are scraped off the cervix and placed on a glass slide to be examined in the laboratory. This scraping is generally done with a wooden spatula, which does not enter the cervix. Occasionally a cotton applicator (Q-tip) or small brush is inserted into the beginning of the opening of the cervix to sample cells from the "endocervix" or cervical lining. Most of these instruments are less than the size that would render her a *niddah* by even the most stringent opinion. In some countries they have introduced a larger brush. A woman should thus check the diameter of the instrument used and convey this information to an authority. It is quite possible for the scraping to cause mild bleeding. However, since this bleeding is due to definite trauma near the external opening of the cervix, unless the instrument is the newer one and the rav is stringent regarding the size, this exam should not render her a *niddah*.

Colposcopy

This is basically a speculum exam with magnification, that allows clearer viewing of the cervix. It is generally done for further evaluation of suspicious findings on the Pap smear or speculum exam. The halachic considerations here are the same as for the speculum exam.

Cervical biopsy

This test is generally done to further investigate abnormal Pap smear and colposcopy results. It consists of grabbing the cervix with an instrument (a tenaculum) and then removing a small portion of the cervix for evaluation. This can definitely cause bleeding. This bleeding is definitely traumatic.

The test itself does not render her a *niddah*. If done during the seven clean days there can be problems with getting valid *bedikot* after the exam has been done. Therefore, it is best not to schedule it at this time. However, if there is no choice, a rabbi should be consulted as to how to proceed.

Endometrial biopsy

An endometrial biopsy, where a small portion of the uterine lining is removed for evaluation, is sometimes performed as part of the work up for unusual bleeding. The purpose is generally to rule out cancer in this location. In this test, a small catheter is inserted into the uterus. The size is generally smaller than the size that would make her a *niddah*. As uterine bleeding will almost definitely be caused by this procedure, the couple should first consult their rabbi to determine whether this bleeding, caused by trauma, will make her a *niddah*.

Vaginal ultrasound

Ultrasound is an invaluable diagnostic tool in gynecology, as it allows visualization of the reproductive organs without x-ray radiation exposure. This test used to be done by placing an external transducer (which emits sound waves) over the abdomen. Recently, examination with a vaginal transducer has become popular for evaluation of many gynecological conditions, as it allows closer "visualization" of the structures of interest. The transducer is about the size of a large tampon. It is inserted into the vagina only, and thus causes no opening of the uterus. It is generally well lubricated and thus unlikely to cause bleeding. Performance of this exam should not render a woman a *niddah*.

Laparoscopy

In this test, a fiber-optic scope is inserted through small abdominal incisions. As the scope does not go through the cervix, there is no issue of cervical dilation. When used for non-gynecological surgery, the woman is not *niddah*. When used for gynecological purposes, all details of the proposed procedure should be obtained and related to a halachic authority to determine its effect on her halachic status.

CHAPTER 2

INFERTILITY[1]

Difficulty in conceiving is a trying situation in any marriage.[2] This is true even more for the halachically observant couple, because of the stress in Jewish law on the commandment to be fruitful and multiply (see the section on birth control, pp. 159–161, for further discussion of this issue). Societal norms in the observant community of having children sooner after marriage, more closely spaced and greater in number than is usual in secular society, add to the pressure. While a full discussion of infertility diagnosis and treatment is beyond the scope of this book, it is important to discuss this topic and its interplay with halacha.

Definition of infertility

About 20% of couples conceive during the first month of trying, and an additional 20% each subsequent month; thus, by six months 86% of couples will have succeeded. General medical practice is to wait until one year of lack of success before initiating a medical evaluation, unless the woman is over 35, in which case the evaluation would start at six months.

---

[1] Further books on this topic:

1) Grazi R. *Overcoming Infertility: A Guide for Jewish Couples*. (Jerusalem: Toby Press, 2005).

2) Finkelstein B. and Finkelstein M. *The Third Key: The Jewish Couple's Guide to Fertility* (Jerusalem: Feldheim, 2005).

[2] Two examples of family strife due to infertility are in the Tanach itself. See Genesis 30:1, 2 for the story of Rachel and Jacob and I Samuel 1:6–8 for the story of Chana and Penina.

These statistics are based on the general population which is often sexually experienced (either due to delaying childbirth after marriage or premarital relations). With the young and previously inexperienced couple,[3] there is reason to allow a few more months before beginning medical evaluation.

Infertility is sometimes divided into two categories – primary, in which no children have been born yet, and secondary, where the couple has already become biological parents but are experiencing difficulty in conceiving further children.

Evaluation of infertility

There are many reasons that can cause a couple difficulty in having children. Some are due to factors in the husband, some are due to factors in the wife, and some are due to both. In order to offer treatment it is important to determine the cause of the problem. This evaluation begins with the taking of a thorough medical history and physical exam of both members of the couple. Two situations, which are often not addressed in the medical literature, need to be taken into consideration in dealing with couples who observe halacha.

Effective marital relations

In dealing with a young couple married for the first time, it is quite important, before embarking on an extensive medical work-up, to verify that sexual relations are taking place in an effective fashion. Exposure to sex is so prevalent in the general community that physicians often assume that their patients know the basics. However, while sex is a natural behavior, it also needs to be learned. Due to concerns with modesty, sex education is often not provided in Jewish education. Availability of sexually explicit literature and media may be limited as well. Essential information about anatomy and physiology should be provided to both members of the couple prior to the wedding as part of teaching the laws of family life (see Appendix C, pp. 200–204). Unfortunately, this is not always the case, and the possibility of the couple having had relations in a manner that will not lead to pregnancy should be delicately explored.

---

[3] Due to the rule of hymenal bleeding making a woman a *niddah*, one to two months can go by before a couple begins having frequent enough intercourse at the time of the month the wife is most likely to conceive.

Halachic infertility

A fertility problem unique to women observing the rules of *niddah* is ovulation prior to immersing in the *mikveh*. The date of ovulation can be determined by a number of methods. One such method is for the woman to measure her temperature before arising every morning ("the basal body temperature"). There is generally a rise of about half a degree Fahrenheit at ovulation. This method can be cumbersome for women who wake at irregular times, and body temperature can be affected by other factors, such as illness. Women can learn to recognize other signs of their fertility as well, such as changes in their cervical discharge.[4] Laboratory tests are also available. One such test is a kit that measures the surge in lutenizing hormone (LH) that precedes ovulation by 12–24 hours. These kits are readily available in pharmacies as "ovulation prediction tests," without a prescription, and can be used in the privacy of one's home. Another method uses serial ultrasounds, which follow the development of the ovarian follicle and can directly record whether ovulation has taken place. Other methods, such as measurement of serum progesterone on approximately day nineteen of the cycle – by when ovulation should have taken place – or biopsy of the uterine lining, can determine that ovulation has taken place, but are less practical regarding timing.

From a medical perspective, the woman who ovulates prior to day twelve of the menstrual cycle but ovulates regularly does not have a fertility problem. However, if because of halacha she cannot have relations until after this point, she will have difficulty conceiving. As mentioned in part one, fertility problems are one reason that even Ashkenazi women would be permitted to wait eleven days rather than twelve, especially if they do not have intercourse right before the onset of their menses.[5] If she ovulates on day 10 or earlier there are other halachic solutions,[6] and a rabbi should be consulted. However, she still needs to have an appropriate *hefsek taharah*,

---

[4] Weschler T. *Taking Charge of Your Fertility: The Definitive Guide to Natural Birth Control, Pregnancy Achievement and Reproductive Health* (New York: Perennial, 2006).

[5] See Ganzel T. and Zimmerman D. *Akarut hilchatit - ivchun vetipul hilchati refu'i.* Assia, 2009; 22:63–81.

[6] *Igrot Moshe* YD 4 17:22.

and thus these solutions only help women who bleed for 2–3 days. For a woman with early ovulation whose menses last five days or longer, the above suggestions do not help.

A woman who suspects she is ovulating before mikveh use should begin by verifying that her menses really last as long as she thinks. Any findings other than bright red on the *hefsek taharah* should be brought to a rabbi to check whether they are, in fact, problematic. The rabbi should be informed that halachic infertility is suspected. If they are, then medications to delay ovulation are often used. These include estrogen, combination estrogen/progesterone and clomiphene citrate. All these medications are prescription only, and should be used under the supervision of a physician.

Halachic solutions, if the medical approaches fail, are more difficult, but exist.[7, 8] A rabbi with experience in this area should be consulted.

Order of diagnostic procedures

The history-taking and physical exam are generally followed by a series of diagnostic tests. As infertility may be due to problems in either spouse, in the general population the examination generally starts simultaneously with the husband and wife. However, as evaluation of the male factors raises more halachic problems,[9] a rabbinic determination should be obtained prior to embarking on this testing. Often rabbis will require that the basic, non-invasive tests be performed on the wife first, and only if these tests do not reveal the cause, then proceed to evaluate the husband. They may also stipulate that a minimum time of marriage without children elapse before permitting such testing.

Evaluation of male factors

Evaluation of male infertility centers around sperm sampling, which requires dealing with the halachic issue of *hotzaat zera lebatalah* (removing semen for naught).

---

[7] *Yabia Omer* 2 EH 1.

[8] Green Y. *"Hazraah Melachutit Kepitaron le Akarut Datit."* *Sefer Assia* 5 (Jerusalem: Machon Schlesinger, 1986) pp. 112–42.

[9] Dichovsky S. *"Bedikot Poriut Vehashlachotehen."* *Techumin* 5758; 18:161–169.

אָסוּר לְהוֹצִיא שִׁכְבַת זֶרַע לְבַטָּלָה. (שולחן ערוך ; אבן העזר, כג:א)

This prohibition of "wasting seed" is a serious consideration. The defini-tion of wasting is the subject of rabbinic debate. There are those who feel that obtaining a semen sample whose eventual purpose is to help fulfill the commandment of procreation does not constitute wasting,[10] while others disagree.

Masturbation to produce a semen sample is a serious halachic problem.[11] Rabbis will often suggest alternate methods that are less prob-lematic. One such method is post-coital testing, where semen is removed from the woman's vagina after intercourse has taken place. As relations have taken place in the natural manner, this does not violate the prohibi-tion of wasting seed. The logistics of a couple having relations just prior to a doctor's appointment is somewhat challenging halachically, because of considerations of modesty and of not having marital relations during the day.[12] However, relations the previous night (about 8 hours before the test) is acceptable. Post-coital testing can provide some information about sperm viability and its interplay with cervical mucus, but cannot be used to evaluate semen volume and other questions. If direct sampling of semen is needed, some rabbis suggest having relations with a condom (with or without a small hole in it) so that, once again, the relations are performed in a natural manner. It should be noted that a special, sterile condom needs to be used for this testing and not the types routinely sold in pharmacies. The hole can be problematic from a medical point of view, as it allows for contamination of the sample being obtained. Each case should be dis-cussed with both the doctor and the rabbi prior to embarking on this testing.

---

[10] *Igrot Moshe* EH 2:16.

[11] *Shulchan Aruch* EH 23:2.

[12] Further discussed in Part Four, chapter 6 (p. 184).

Evaluation of female factors

Hysterogram or Hysterosalpingogram (HSG)

Done in order to look for anatomic abnormalities in the uterus, this test consists of inserting a small catheter into the uterus, injecting a radio-opaque dye and taking an x-ray picture. A similar test is done by injecting water and evaluating the uterus by ultrasound – a sono-hysterogram (SHG) or saline hysterosynography. In both tests the catheter is generally smaller (<3mm) than that which would render her a *niddah* (but one should ask to be sure). Bleeding from this procedure may be due to irritation to the uterus by the catheter, and thus would be *dam makkah* (bleeding due to injury) and not *dam niddah* (uterine bleeding that would render her a *niddah*). As there are different halachic approaches to such bleeding, the couple should consult a rabbi. It should be noted that for the HSG a colored dye is used and the cervix is cleaned with betadine which is brown; thus, stains other than blood can be expected to appear.

Hysteroscopy

Also done to look for anatomic abnormalities, and sometimes to treat them if found,[13] this test consists of inserting a fiber-optic scope to view the inside of the uterus. The physician can actually view whether trauma has resulted from the scope. The size of the scope and whether bleeding was seen should be reported to the rabbi. The cervix is often grabbed with a tenaculum, which commonly causes bleeding whose origin is the outside of the cervix.

Endometrial biopsy

As part of a work-up for infertility, an endometrial biopsy is sometimes performed to evaluate the status of the lining of the uterus. This test is discussed in Part Four, chapter 1 (p. 148).

---

[13] Such as a lysis of adhesions, the breaking up of tissue in places it does not belong.

Infertility Treatment

The treatment available depends on the suspected underlying cause. Cases of hormonal imbalance are treated with medication. Simple obstructions of the male or female reproductive tracts are treated with surgery. Sometimes testing and/or treatment involves testicular biopsy or surgery. Any surgery on the reproductive organs of the male may involve the serious halachic problem of damaging male reproductive organs. Certain such situations could forbid further physical relations on the part of the couple. A rabbi with experience in this field, working in concert with a physician sensitive to the halachic needs of the patient, should be consulted to determine the best halachic approach to each individual situation.[14]

For treatment of complicated problems such as insufficient sperm, procurement of semen samples may be required. This raises the same concerns as those for obtaining a sample for testing (see above). Since the purpose is to allow the fulfillment of the commandment to be fruitful and multiply, and not "wasting," many authorities permit such procurement.

Assisted Reproductive Technology (ART) consists of a series of procedures in which the fertilization is assisted by medical intervention:

Artificial insemination (AI)[15] involves placing sperm in the vaginal canal and allowing it to proceed up the cervix the same way it would naturally. Medically, this can be done with donor (AID) or husband (AIH) sperm. Donor sperm raises very serious halachic concerns. The obligation of be fruitful and multiply is incumbent on the husband, and use of donor sperm does not fulfill his obligation. Some authorities even maintain that it is the equivalent of adultery and that the resulting child would be a *mamzer* with its disastrous ramifications. Others do not agree, but nevertheless do not permit the procedure. Artificial insemination with the husband's sperm

---

[14] See *Proceedings of the First International Conference on Medicine, Ethics and Halacha* (Jerusalem: Machon Schlesinger, 1993) pp. 125–145.

[15] For further discussion see: 1) Cohen A.S. "Artificial Insemination." *Journal of Halacha and Contemporary Society* 1987; 13:43–60. 2) Steinberg A. "*Hazraa Melachutit Leor Hahalacha.*" *Sefer Assia* 1 (Jerusalem: Machon Schlesinger, 1983).

is less problematic, but still raises the issues of procurement of sperm that were discussed above.

Intra-uterine injection (IUI) of washed sperm is done in cases where it is felt that cervical barriers are leading to the lack of success in achieving pregnancy. As in the natural process, the sperm need to swim to the fallopian tube for conception to occur. In **transuterine tubal insemination (TUTI)** the washed sperm are placed directly in the fallopian tube, obviating the need for them to find their own way there. The halachic considerations in these procedures are those of procuring the sperm, as discussed under testing, and the insertion of instruments into the uterus as discussed under the hysterogram.

In vitro fertilization (IVF) takes place in a petri dish, and the ensuing product is injected into the reproductive tract. In classic IVF the pre-embryo is placed into the uterus on about day 3 (8 cell stage) or day 5–6 (blastocyst transfer). The theoretical drawback is that the embryo reaches the uterus at a much "younger" stage than it would in natural conception. To supercede this problem, procedures have been developed to place the products of conception in the fallopian tube and allow maturation to take place there. In **gamete interfallopian transfer (GIFT)** the pre-embryo is placed; in **zygote interfallopian transfer (ZIFT)** a later stage (zygote) is placed. The latter two procedures require laparoscopy which is more invasive than egg retrieval, which is done trans-vaginally. Therefore most ART in the United States is IVF.

These procedures raise the issues of procurement of sperm, insertion of instruments into the uterus and a large number of "halachic-medical ethics" issues:

1. Does IVF fulfill the commandment to be fruitful and multiply? It is a matter of rabbinical debate whether this commandment applies to any production of offspring, or only to conception of children as a result of normal sexual relations.[16] If the latter, then not only would IVF not fulfill

---

[16] Waldenberg Y. *"Hafrayat Mavchenah – Diyun Refu'i Hilchati." Sefer Assia* 5 (Jerusalem: Machon Schlesinger, 1986).

the commandment, there would be less justification for permitting procurement of semen for the procedure.

2. Status of the embryos so produced. In general, more embryos are produced than are subsequently implanted. The remainder can be frozen for future use. When the couple does not desire any further children, from a halachic point of view they can be destroyed.[17]

3. Ensuring parenthood. After the sperm and eggs are removed from the respective bodies of the parents, the possibility of lab error exists which would have serious halachic implications as to the identity of the child. While all labs take precautions to avoid this, mix-ups have happened. To prevent this, some IVF labs hire a halachic supervisor to ensure that only the appropriate egg and sperm are joined, and also that any remaining sperm, ova or embryos are not used for other couples.

When the mother is not able to produce an ovum for use in IVF, ovum donation is sometimes considered. This raises questions of who is the halachic mother.[18] Similar concerns are raised by surrogacy.

Support
As in other stressful situations, peer support can be helpful to the couple experiencing infertility. The largest organization dealing with this topic is RESOLVE, which has chapters throughout the United States.[19]

---

[17] Eliyahu M. "*Hashmadat Beiziot Vedilul Ubarim.*" *Techumin* 5754; 14:272–274.

[18] For further reading see:

1) Bleich J.D. *Contemporary Halachic Problems* Vol IV (NY: Ktav, 1995) pp. 237–272.

2) Goldberg N. "*Yechus Imahut Beshtelat Ubar Berechem Shel Acheret.*" *Techumin* 5745; 5:248–259.

3) Kilav A.Y. "*Mihu Imo Shel Yilod Hahorah o Hayoledet.*" *Techumin* 5745; 5:260–267.

4) Ariel Y. "*Hafrayah Melachutit Upundakaut.*" *Techumin* 5756; 16:171–80.

In Israel there is a similar organization known as *Tinok Shebalev*.[20] Specifically for the Jewish religious couple there is a newsletter A T.I.M.E.[21] In Israel Machon Puah assists couples both in negotiating the medical-halachic issues involved and providing support.[22] Zir Chemed also specializes in sensitive treatment of religious couples experiencing infertility.[23]

---

[19] RESOLVE, 1310 Broadway, Sommerville, Mass 02144-1731, phone (617) 623-1156, fax (617) 623-0252, HelpLine (617) 623-0744, www.resolve.org.

[20] Children of My Heart, pob 4047, Jerusalem, Israel 91040, phone 972-2-563-7479, fax 972-2-563-7483, tinok@netvision.net.il.

[21] A T.I.M.E., 1312 44th Street, P.O.B. 132, Brooklyn, NY 11219, HelpLine (718) 437-7110, ATIME@atime.org.

[22] PUAH Institute, Rechov Azriel 19, Jerusalem, Israel, phone 972-2-6515050, fax 972-2-6517501, info@puah.org.il, www.puah.org.il.

[23] Zir Chemed's address is not advertised by the organization, to further protect privacy of clients, phone 972-2-653-6859.

CHAPTER 3

BIRTH CONTROL

There are a number of halachic issues involved in the use of birth control: Is birth control permitted? Under what circumstances? Which methods are preferable?

Is birth control permitted?

Having children is considered a goal of creation (*Eduyot* 1:13).

וַיְבָרֶךְ אֹתָם אֱלֹקִים וַיֹּאמֶר לָהֶם אֱלֹקִים פְּרוּ וּרְבוּ וּמִלְאוּ אֶת הָאָרֶץ וְכִבְשֻׁהָ.

"And the Lord blessed them, and the Lord said to them, be fruitful and multiply, and conquer the land..."

From this blessing in Genesis 1:28 is derived the biblical commandment to "be fruitful and multiply." Technically, this commandment applies to men and not women.[1] Since today men are only allowed to have one wife, this obligation de facto applies to the wife as well, but on the lower level of enabling her husband to fulfill the commandment.[2]

לֹא יִבָּטֵל אָדָם מִפְּרִיָה וְרִבְיָה – אֶלָּא אִם כֵּן יֶשׁ לוֹ בָנִים. בֵּית שַׁמַּאי אוֹמְרִים: שְׁנֵי זְכָרִים, וּבֵית הַלֵּל אוֹמְרִים: זָכָר וּנְקֵבָה. (משנה; יבמות, ו:ו)

---

[1] Rambam, *Hilchot Ishut* 15:2

הָאִישׁ מְצֻוֶּה עַל פְּרִיָה וְרִבְיָה אֲבָל לֹא הָאִשָּׁה.

[2] There are those who also feel that the rabbinic commandment of "*lashevet*," mentioned below, obligates women.

A man should not desist from procreation unless he has children. The house of Shammai says these are two sons, the house of Hillel says these are a son and a daughter.
(Mishna *Yevamot* 6:6)

The biblical commandment is defined by halacha, following the opinion of Hillel, as having one son and one daughter who themselves reproduce. There also exists a rabbinic admonishment not to desist from being involved in procreation.

אַף עַל פִּי שֶׁקִיֵּים אָדָם מִצְוַת פְּרִיָּה וּרְבִיָּה, הֲרֵי הוּא מְצֻוֶּה מִדִּבְרֵי סוֹפְרִים שֶׁלֹּא יִבָּטֵל מִלִּפְרוֹת וְלִרְבּוֹת כָּל זְמַן שֶׁיֶּשׁ בּוֹ כֹּחַ, שֶׁכָּל הַמּוֹסִיף נֶפֶשׁ אַחַת בְּיִשְׂרָאֵל כְּאִילּוּ בָּנָה עוֹלָם. (רמב״ם; הלכות אישות טו:טז)

Even though one has fulfilled the commandment to be fruit-ful and multiply, it is a Rabbinic commandment not to desist from procreation as long as he has strength, because one who adds one soul to Israel is as if he has built a world....
(Rambam, *Hilchot Ishut* 15:16)

This is often tied to the verse in Ecclesiastes 11:6:

בַּבֹּקֶר זְרַע אֶת זַרְעֶךָ וְלָעֶרֶב אַל תַּנַּח יָדֶךָ כִּי אֵינְךָ יוֹדֵעַ אֵי זֶה יִכְשָׁר הֲזֶה אוֹ זֶה וְאִם שְׁנֵיהֶם כְּאֶחָד טוֹבִים.

In the morning sow your seed and in the evening do not desist, for you do not know which will succeed or whether both will be equally good.

The verse in Isaiah 45:18 is sometimes connected with this as well.

כִּי כֹה אָמַר ד', בּוֹרֵא הַשָּׁמַיִם הוּא הָאֱלֹקִים יֹצֵר הָאָרֶץ וְעֹשָׂהּ הוּא כוֹנְנָהּ לֹא תֹהוּ בְרָאָהּ לָשֶׁבֶת יְצָרָהּ אֲנִי ד' וְאֵין עוֹד.

So says God Creator of the heavens, He is the Lord who fashioned the earth; He established it not to remain a void but to settle it.

The exact definition and parameters of this obligation are the subject of much discussion. There is room in Jewish law for birth control, in certain circumstances. The most obvious is when the mother's life is in danger, following the principle that danger to life suspends all the commandments other than adultery, idolatry, and murder. Other issues, such as the mother's physical condition, emotional condition and the family's ability to cope, can be taken into consideration as well. There is also room for leniency to allow a mother to recuperate from childbirth and provide spacing of children.[3] A full discussion of this topic is beyond the scope of the book.[4] Each couple's individual circumstances should be discussed with a rabbinic authority.

What is the preferred method?

Once the decision has been made that delaying pregnancy is permissible under the circumstances, the next question is which method is preferable. This involves a number of issues. As mentioned previously (pp.152–153),

---

[3] *Bnei Banim* Vol 2 number 38. *Shut Siach Nahum. Even HaEzer* 94.

[4] Suggested readings include:

1) Schachter H. "Halachic Aspects of Family Planning," in *Halacha and Contemporary Society* (New York: Ktav, 1984) pp. 3–30.

2) Steinberg A. *"Hagishah Hayehudit Haklalit Lemeniat Herayon." Sefer Assia* 3 (Jerusalem: Machon Schlesinger, 1983).

3) Aviner S.C. *"Tichnun Mishpachah Vemeniat Herayon." Sefer Assia* 3 (Jerusalem: Machon Schlesinger, 1983).

4) *Bnei Banim* Vol 2 number 38.

5) Katane Y, Katan C, Bar-On A. *"Emtza'eh Meni'ah – Mabat Refui Hilchati" Assia* 5754; 14:114–123.

6) Steinberg A. *Encyclopedia Hilchatit Refu'it.* (Jerusalem: Machon Schlesinger, 1988) s.v. *meneyat herayon.*

Note that not all possible situations are listed. Thus, if the couple feels the need to delay pregnancy, a question should be asked. The answer should not be assumed in advance.

emission of semen outside the vaginal canal and not in the process of intercourse, *hotzaat zera lebatalah*, is a halachic problem. Therefore methods that allow marital relations in the most normal manner (כדרך כל הארץ) are the most preferable.

Surgical sterilization is not an acceptable method. Leviticus 22:24 states:

וּמָעוּךְ וְכָתוּת וְנָתוּק וְכָרוּת לֹא תַקְרִיבוּ לַד' וּבְאַרְצְכֶם לֹא תַעֲשׂוּ.

This verse not only states that one cannot bring a sacrifice of an animal whose genitalia have been damaged, but that one is also prohibited to inflict such damage. As stated in the *Shuchan Aruch*[5]:

אָסוּר לְהַפְסִיד אֶבְרֵי הַזֶּרַע, בֵּין בְּאָדָם בֵּין בִּבְהֵמָה חַיָּה וְעוֹף, אֶחָד טְמֵאִים וְאֶחָד טְהוֹרִים, בֵּין בְּאֶרֶץ יִשְׂרָאֵל בֵּין בְּחוּץ לָאָרֶץ... וְהַמְסָרֵס אֶת הַנְּקֵבָה, בֵּין בְּאָדָם בֵּין בִּשְׁאָר מִינִים, פָּטוּר אֲבָל אָסוּר.

This prohibits the sterilization of men and animals. By most opinions, it is a biblical prohibition for men and a rabbinic prohibition for women.

This prohibition of *sirus* refers, by most opinions, to a permanent and stable condition and not to a temporary state. Vasectomy and tubal ligation are permanent forms of birth control and thus raise serious problems with *sirus*. Vasectomy is a biblically prohibited form of birth control. Tubal ligation ("tying the tubes") or insertion of coils is a rabbinic prohibition and would only be permitted under dire circumstances.[6, 7, 8]

One method of birth control for a limited time that has no halachic problems at all is the lactational amenorrhea method. This method, which capitalizes on the anovulation brought on by breastfeeding, states that up

---

[5] *Shulchan Aruch* EH 5:11.

[6] Ozarowski J.S. *"Tubal Ligation and Jewish Law: an Overview." Journal of Halacha and Contemporary Society.* 1984; 7:42–52.

[7] Malach D. *"Ikur Chatzotzrot." Sefer Assia* 8. (Jerusalem: Machon Schlesinger, 1995).

[8] Now that a tubal ligation can sometimes be reversed (although with variable success), or pregnancy can still occur with the use of IVF, there are those who are somewhat more lenient.

to six months postpartum, if the woman has not resumed menses and is exclusively or almost exclusively breastfeeding, her risk of pregnancy is less than 1%.[9] This has been proven effective in multiple clinical trials world-wide, including in developed countries, and has the added health benefits that are accrued to mother and infant by breastfeeding. As discussed in Part Two (p. 135), the halacha encourages breastfeeding for at least two years, without concern about the potential reduction in fecundity at this time.[10]

Whether or not a woman is breastfeeding, knowing when she ovulates can be used to time marital relations to avoid pregnancy. This method is known as fertility awareness. Women can be taught to recognize three signs of ovulation – changes in body temperature upon arising, in the position of the cervix, and in the nature of cervical secretions. When all three signs are used by a properly trained woman, this method can be as effective as 95-97%.

This method may be used by couples for whom delaying pregnancy is halachically permitted. It should be noted, however, that its use by women who keep *hilchot niddah* markedly decreases the number of days available for marital relations. *Mikveh* night is likely to come out on a fertile day. It is permissible to avoid having relations on *mikveh* night if both husband and wife agree. If it is hard to be *tehorah* and not have relations, it is permissible to delay *mikveh* immersion. However, until immersion all *halachot* of *niddah* have to be observed.

---

[9] See: 1) The World Health Organization. "Multinational Study of Breastfeeding and Lactational Amenorrhea (Parts I and II)." *Fertility and Sterility* 1998; 70:450–471.

2) Labbok M.H., Perez A., Valdes F. et al. "The Lactational Amenorrhea Method (LAM): A Postpartum Introductory Family Planning Method with Policy and Program Implications." *Advances in Contraception* 1994; 10:93–109.

3) Short R.V., Lexis P.R., Renfree M.B. Shaw G. "Contraceptive Effects of Extended Lactational Amenorrhoea: Beyond the Bellagio Consensus." *Lancet* 1991; 337:715–17.

4) Kennedy K.I, Visness C.M. "Contraceptive Efficacy of Lactational Amenorrhoea." *Lancet* 1992; 339:227–29

5) Lewis P.R., Brown J.B., Renfree M.B., Short R.V. "The Resumption of Ovulation and Menstruation in a Well Nourished Population of Women Breastfeeding for an Extended Period of Time." *Fertility and Sterility* 1991; 55:529–36.

[10] *Bnei Banim* Vol 1 number 31.

Hormonal regulation is usually the birth-control method of first choice, as it is more than 99% effective, is temporary and provides no physical barriers to intercourse. Some rabbis hesitate to recommend this method due to health concerns.[11] With the modern low-dose estrogen preparations available, the risks for most women are negligible. Some women however, have medical conditions (liver disease, high blood pressure, clotting problems) that preclude their use. All women should be seen by a physician and undergo an appropriate history and physical exam before beginning hormonal contraception. A follow up exam after 1–2 months of use to check blood pressure is also recommended.

There are two categories of hormonal contraception. Most common are the oral pills that consist of a combination of estrogen and progesterone that are given for a fixed time and then interrupted to allow for shedding of the uterine lining to take place.[12] Similar formulations to the "pill" are now available in the form of a patch and an intravaginal ring. The other category is progesterone-only formulations. They are available in oral form ("the mini pill") taken daily, as an injection (Depo Provera) given every three months, or as a subcutaneous implant that lasts several years.[13] Progesterone-only formulations are favored by some physicians for use while breastfeeding, as they are reported to have less effect on milk production.

These same medications can be used in a different dosage to prevent pregnancy after marital relations. This is known as emergency contraception or "the morning after pill". It is intended for use when a problem has occurred with another form of contraception (such as forgetting to use it). It can cause significant side effects (such as nausea) and is not meant for regular use. From a halachic point of view, it is less preferable than ongoing hormonal contraception, as it prevents implantation rather than fertilization. This, according to some, is a form of abortion, as discussed below

---

[11] *Shut Siach Nahum. Even HaEzer* 95.

[12] There are formulations that advertise withdrawal bleeding as infrequently as once a year. However it should be noted that there is a higher incidence of breakthrough bleeding which could render a woman *niddah*.

[13] To the best of my knowledge, no specific responsa have been written about the implant. It is likely that it would be somewhat less preferable due to the length of its action, unless there are clear circumstances that warrant such a long interruption of fertility.

regarding the IUD. However, as the woman is not sure that she has conceived and this abortion would be extremely early in pregnancy, most authorities would permit the use of emergency contraception when needed.

The method that is next-in-line as far as the naturalness of the relations is the intra-uterine device (IUD). This consists of a small device inserted into the uterus. Two small strings are left protruding from the cervix to enable confirmation that the device is still in place and to facilitate removal. The exact mechanism of this device is still not completely understood. The currently accepted theory is that the copper containing IUDs cause a reaction of the uterus to a foreign body. This in turn kills the sperm and prevents living sperm from reaching the fallopian tubes where fertilization takes place.[14, 15] The older theory is that the IUD prevents implantation of the already formed embryo in the uterine lining. This second theory is also true, as post-coital insertion of an IUD up to one week after intercourse has been shown to effectively prevent conception. However, this is now considered primarily a back up mechanism rather than the main form of action.

The different theories have halachic implications as to the desirability of this form of contraception. If the primary mechanism is preventing fertilization, this presents few halachic problems in a situation where contraception is permissible. On the other hand, if implantation is what is prevented, then the issue of abortion is raised.[16] However, in the minority of cases where this may occur, we are dealing with a very early abortion long before forty days after conception.[17]

There were cases of death associated with the use of one brand of IUD, which lead to the banning of this method for a number of years in the United States. Other brands are now available. The main concern with

---

[14] Kaunitz A.M. "Reappearance of the Intrauterine Device." *International Journal of Fertility* 1997; 42:120–7.

[15] Ortiz M.E, Croxatto H.B., Bardin C.W. "Mechanism of Action of Intrauterine Devices." *Obstetric Gynecologic Survey* 1996; 51:S42–51.

[16] For continued debate see:

Katane Y., Katan C. *"Chashash Hapalah Beikvot Hetken Toch Rechmi Veshimush Begluglot Etzel Nashim Mevugarot." Assia* 5759; 15:165–168 and the response of Levi U. in that volume, pp. 167–169.

[17] See section on abortion (p. 181).

this method is a fear of increasing pelvic inflammatory disease, which can lead to sterility. Thus, some physicians will only use it in women who already have their desired number of children. For monogamous women the danger from this method is slight. Nevertheless, since preserving health is a serious concern of Jewish law, some rabbis do not recommend this method.

The diaphragm is a latex cup placed deep inside the vagina near the cervix. It holds spermicidal gel or foam, and physically blocks entry of the sperm into the cervix. There is a discussion in the Talmud about whether women who are at risk if they become pregnant are allowed or required to use a *moch*.[18] There is debate among the *Rishonim* as to whether this was a device that was present at the time of intercourse, or a form of sponge that was inserted afterwards to absorb the semen. There is also debate as to what are the implications for all the other women not mentioned in the Talmud – are they permitted or forbidden to use a *moch*? Some rabbis compare a diaphragm to a *moch* and forbid it except in dire circumstances. Others feel that the diaphragm is different because it is inserted deeply and the husband is rarely aware that it is present; it thus enables normal relations and is permissible.[19, 20] A similar but little used method is the cervical cap, where a cap is placed over the cervix.

Spermicides, although they kill sperm, are not considered "wasting seed" and do not interfere with natural relations.[21] For this reason many authorities permit their use although there are those who find them objectionable.[22] However, their use alone without a diaphragm is not a very effective method of birth control (about 75% efficacy) and thus not helpful in cases where pregnancy MUST be avoided. They are sometimes of use as a backup method for women who are otherwise unlikely to get pregnant

---

[18] *Yevamot* 12b, *Ketubot* 37a and 39a, *Niddah* 3a.

[19] *Bnei Banim* Vol 1 number 30.

[20] *Shut Siach Nahum* Even Haezer 94.

[21] Spermicides found in a contraceptive sponge may be more problematic as the sponge occupies a small part of the vaginal canal and thus raises similar issues to the diaphragm.

[22] See discussion in *Nishmat Avraham* EH I:15.

(e.g., breastfeeding women) or for whom a pregnancy would not be catastrophic.

Since the obligation to be fruitful and multiply is incumbent by biblical law on the man, methods that involve the husband are more problematic. A hormonal contraceptive used by men[23] would thus be more problematic than a hormonal contraceptive used by women. Use of a condom is very problematic from the point of view of "wasting" semen. In situations where there is no other option, such as exposure to HIV, a rabbinic opinion should be sought.

Effects of specific methods on *hilchot niddah*

Hormonal contraception

Hormonal contraceptives present an interesting halachic situation. While taking the pills, the woman is unlikely to bleed. She will start to bleed a few days after she stops taking active pills. In general, use of hormonal contraception is arranged so a woman has a 28-day cycle; she takes active hormones for 21 days – either the same pill, a series of pills in fluctuating doses of estrogen and progesterone, a weekly patch or an intravaginal ring. She then stops taking the medication for a week, resulting in a very regular 28-day cycle. These 28 days are convenient for medical calculations, but are simply a matter of convention. A woman should discuss with her doctor the possibility of taking the active pills for slightly longer in order to result in a longer cycle and relatively fewer days as a *niddah*. In cases of upcoming vacation or travel, a physician can also be consulted to see if she can delay her menses for a short period. There are newer formulations that are designed a priori to have menses every number of months. Anecdotally, however, they seem more likely to produce breakthrough bleeding. Most formulations provide for stopping active medication to allow for shedding of the uterine lining.

The halachic consequences of taking artificial hormones are a matter of debate. Some halachic authorities were so concerned with irregular

---

23 Not yet on the market, but currently undergoing clinical testing.

bleeding that they either questioned the permissibility of the method[24] or required a month of abstinence[25] or an internal exam prior to all relations.[26] This does not seem to be the widely accepted view today, perhaps because, with the more modern formulations, less irregular bleeding is expected.

There is also rabbinic debate on the effect of the hormones on the rules of the *onot prishah*. Some authorities rule that a woman continues to keep her usual *vestot* regardless of the fact that she is taking hormones, there are those who calculate based only on the hormonal contraceptive, and there are those who impose the stringencies of both.[27, 28] A woman should consult with her rabbi about how to proceed.

It should be noted that progesterone-only preparations are more likely to cause problems with spotting that could render a woman a *niddah*. The injectable form is particularly problematic as it continues its effect for at least three months, and so if a woman has problems of this nature they can continue even after the contraceptive effect of the medication wears off.

The patch and the ring formulations raise questions of removal in order to immerse in the *mikveh*. *Mikveh* use will generally be at that time of the cycle that these devices are meant to be worn. Removal of the ring for up to two hours does not affect its contraceptive properties and thus it can simply be removed just prior to immersion and then re-inserted. If inadvertently forgotten, it would not require re-immersion. The active ingredient of the patch is found in the glue. Therefore, it would probably be best to replace the patch with a new one after its removal for immersion. This, however, increases the cost of this birth control method. Some gynecologists feel that as long as the patch still sticks unaided it remains effective. A woman should check with her own physician.

---

[24] *Bnei Banim* Vol 1 number 30.

[25] *Igrot Moshe* EH 1:65.

[26] *Igrot Moshe* EH 3:24, 4:72.

[27] Levi S. "*Hashpa'at Hashimush Beglulot al Din Vestot.*" *Techumin* 5743; 3:179–85.

[28] Adler S. "*Hashpa'at Hashimush Beglulot al Din Vestot.*" *Techumin* 5744; 4:461–3.

Intrauterine Device (IUD)

a. insertion

Placing the IUD requires grasping of the cervix to stabilize it and inserting the device, generally with the assistance of an introducer. The issues here are similar to those discussed above concerning the hysterogram. The size of the introducer should be determined. It is generally smaller than 19 mm and so does not cause the degree of opening that would render her a *niddah*. Some bleeding can result from the grasping of the cervix. Depending on the time of her cycle this would probably not render her a *niddah*, as it can be attributed to trauma, but a rabbinical authority should be consulted.[29]

b. removal

Removing the IUD requires grasping the strings that are attached and protrude from the cervix, and pulling. This generally leads to a sensation of cramping and may be accompanied by some trauma-related bleeding. Depending on the time of her cycle this would probably not render her a *niddah*, but a rabbinical authority should be consulted.

c. irregular bleeding

The main drawback to IUD use by women who keep the laws of *niddah* is that this method is likely to cause extra bleeding. This can either be heavier menses or irregular bleeding. Heavy menses result in additional days of staining before she can do a *hefsek taharah*. Irregular bleeding can cancel out the blood-free days that she has counted so far, leading to prolonged periods of being a *niddah*, or can make her a *niddah* again soon after immersing in the *mikveh*. Women using this method should definitely wear colored underwear to prevent being a *niddah* more than necessary. There are those who argue that this irregular bleeding should not render her a *niddah* at all, as it is due to the trauma of the device on the uterine lining.[30,31] Most rabbis do not, at present, accept this view.[32] However, if she encounters problems she should consult a rabbi before abandoning the method.

---

[29] Pris Y. *"Hetken Toch Rechmi Vetzilum Rechem."* Techumin 5755; 15:332–47.

[30] Levi U. *"Dimum Mechamat Chadirat Hetken Toch Rechmi,"* Assia 5759; 17:145–7

[31] Levi U. *"Bein Dam Ledam,"* Assia 5753; 8:19–22.

[32] Halperin M. *"Dimum Mechamat Hetken Toch Rechmi – Mabat Refu'i Hilchati,"* Assia 5749; 17:138–143.

One type of IUD includes progesterone. This is marketed as causing less bleeding. It does, in fact, result in fewer problems of heavy menses and the resulting anemia, but produces a friable uterine lining that is more likely to stain. In addition, since the medication that is part of this device can cause bleeding due to hormonal changes in the lining, even those who view the intermenstrual bleeding from a plain IUD as resulting from trauma would not do so in this case. Women choosing this method should be prepared for several difficult months at the beginning.

Since the IUD is inserted deeply (inside the uterus), it is considered *balua* ("swallowed"), and neither it nor the strings that extrude into the vagina are considered a barrier in using the *mikveh*.[33]

Diaphragm

A diaphragm contains no hormones and does not enter the uterus, so it has no direct effect on menstruation. However, when removing the diaphragm sometimes blood is noticed on the device. While this may conceivably be due to scratching oneself on removal, since the diaphragm is deep within the vagina it is hard to attribute blood on it to sources from outside the uterus. Since insertion is similar to doing an internal exam, there are those who apply to it the more stringent criteria that are applied to a *bedikah* cloth: she may have had a halachic sensation of which she was unaware, and thus the question has to be considered on a possible biblical level. Nevertheless, if there is only a slight amount of blood and she felt that she scratched herself, she should ask a rabbinic question.[34] It is best not to look at the diaphragm prior to washing after use.

The diaphragm is meant to be removed, generally, six or more hours after use and would not be in place when going to the *mikveh*; leaving it in place for too long is dangerous because of toxic shock syndrome. If inadvertently it was left in place during immersion, a question should be asked whether she needs to immerse again.

---

[33] *Tzitz Eliezer* 11:63.

[34] *Igrot Moshe* YD 4:17(16).

CHAPTER 4

MEDICAL CONDITIONS

Menstrual disorders

Any deviation from a predictable pattern has obvious implications for *hilchot niddah*. In order to understand the technical language used by doctors in describing these conditions, the common classes of abnormal uterine bleeding and their definitions are:[1]

> 1. Oligomenorrhea – bleeding at intervals of greater than 40 days. This type of bleeding is generally irregular. Of halachic note is that women with fairly regular periods that are always longer than 30 days may, according to some opinions, be able to observe fewer than usual days of separation. This situation should be discussed with a rabbi.

> 2. Polymenorrhea – bleeding at intervals of less than 22 days, that may be regular or irregular. This situation is likely to result in the halachic infertility discussed above (pp.151–152).

> 3. Menorrhagia – bleeding that is excessive in both amount and duration, at regular intervals.

---

[1] C.B. Hammond and D.H. Riddick. "Menstruation and Disorders of Menstrual Function" in *Danforth's Obstetrics and Gynecology 8th ed* (Philadilphia: Lippincott William and Wilkins, 1998).

4. Metrorrhagia – bleeding in the usual amount, but at irregular intervals.

5. Menometrorrhagia – bleeding that is excessive and prolonged, either regular or irregular.

6. Hypomenorrhea – bleeding less than the usual amount, at regular intervals.

7. Intermenstrual bleeding – bleeding that occurs between what are otherwise normal menstrual periods.

8. Amenorrhea – absence of menstruation. If a girl has never menstruated by age 16 this is known as primary amenorrhea. No menses for at least 12 months post menarche is classified as secondary amenorrhea.

The implications of menstrual abnormalities are:

1. Problems that involve excessive or prolonged bleeding can (a) markedly increase the time a woman is in the *niddah* status, and (b) lead to anemia.

2. Problems of irregular bleeding can (a) be an indication of problems that will also manifest themselves as fertility problems, and (b) if a woman is truly very irregular, she may be halachically required to do an internal exam before all intercourse. Each individual situation should be discussed with a rabbi.

Unexpected bleeding

Apparent uterine bleeding not at the expected time of menstruation can be from a number of causes. They can be divided into various causes:

Causes outside the reproductive tract:

Hematuria

Blood in the urine can cause questions of *niddah*, as one needs to verify that the bleeding is not uterine. A doctor should be consulted for the source of the bleeding (which is usually something simple, like a urinary tract infection) and then a rabbinic opinion sought. It should be remembered that certain foods such as beets can give the urine a reddish hue.

Hematochezia

Blood in the stool can be the result of many factors such as infections, parasites, hemorrhoids or even cancer. If it is <u>clear</u> that it is from a rectal source, she is not a *niddah*. If it is only <u>possible</u> that it is from a rectal source she still may not be a *niddah*, depending when in her cycle she sees the blood. She should consult a rabbi as to her *niddah* status. As blood in stool may have serious medical consequences she should consult a physician as well, especially women over age 40 when the possibility of rectal cancer increases.

External injury

Blood from external injury — lacerations, abrasions, irritation — does not make a woman a *niddah*. Thus, if a woman experiences bleeding from the genital area that is not from her menses, she can look with a mirror to see if she sees any of the above. If she cannot see them herself but she suspects they are there (for example, it hurts or burns) she should consult a physician for an examination. If the bleeding is clearly from the injury she is not a *niddah*. Even if it is possible that the bleeding is from there, this would not make her a *niddah* during much of the month, and she should consult a rabbi.

Causes inside the reproductive tract include:

Irritation of the vagina

Hypoestrogen

When the vaginal lining is thin it is more likely to bleed from minor irritation. This happens when estrogen levels are low such as during the early part of the menstrual cycle. It is also common while taking hormonal contraception, while breastfeeding and after menopause. Local lubricants, and sometimes locally applied estrogen can often help.

Infections

Infection of the vaginal canal can cause irritation and minor bleeding. The causes can be bacterial or fungal. The treatment depends on the cause.

Foreign bodies

Women sometimes forget items such as tampons and diaphragms in the vaginal canal. These may present themselves as bleeding from the ensuing irritation.

Conditions of the cervix

Ectropion[2]

The inside of the cervical canal is lined with one-cell deep columnar epithelium which is thin and fragile. The outside of the cervix is covered with a number of layers of squamous epithelium, which is thicker and more resilient. In a number of situations such as post-childbirth, the internal type of lining can be found on the outside of the cervix, as well. This is known

---

[2] Katane Y., Katane C., *Petzaim Betzavar Harechem – Hebet Refu'i Hilchati. Techumin* 5755; 15:316–331. In this article Rabbi Y Katane and Dr. C Katane distinguish between ectropion, which does not bleed and erosion, which does. Other gynecological sources do not make this distinction. If the physician can show that minor touch leads to bleeding, then the exact medical category is not important in enabling halachic determination.

as ectropion. When asymptomatic, it is not a medical problem. However, this area is friable and can bleed when touched during internal examination or during intercourse. If such a lesion is found by a physician, he can see if it is currently bleeding or if it bleeds when touched with a cotton swab. This information should be conveyed to a rabbi to decide whether the bleeding can be attributed to this lesion and thus not render her a *niddah*.

Cervicitis

Cervicitis is inflammation of the cervix. It can be caused by a number of pathogens. If the doctor makes this diagnosis, ask whether the lesion is bleeding or could bleed. This information should be passed on to a rabbi to decide if the bleeding can be attributed to the lesion and thus not render her a *niddah*.

Benign pelvic growths

Fibroids

Fibroids, or uterine leiomyoma, are very common benign tumors of muscle tissue that are found in the uterus. They can be found on the outer surface of the uterus (subserosal), within the wall of the uterus (intramural) or under the inner lining of the uterus (submucousal). Only about 25% are symptomatic. The first two generally present themselves as abdominal masses. The last can distort the endometrial lining and produce abnormal uterine bleeding – generally prolonged heavy menses – and its attendant questions related to the laws of *niddah*. The frequency of these growths increases as a woman moves through her reproductive years and is highest in the peri-menopausal period. They generally shrink naturally at menopause.

Treatment is available if fibroids are symptomatic or extremely large. Treatment with a number of hormones whose goal is to induce a menopausal-like state is sometimes employed for temporary improvement, although with this treatment they are likely to recur. Newer treatments include attempting to shrink the fibroid with ultrasound waves under MRI guidance or reducing the fibroid's blood supply by uterine artery embolization. The method used for women past childbearing who are not candidates for or do not desire other methods is removal of the uterus (hysterectomy).[3]

Polyps

Polyps are benign growths. They can occur on the endometrium where they can cause intermenstrual spotting. They can occur on the cervix where they present themselves as post-coital bleeding. It is generally possible to remove them to help solve the bleeding problem. If it is felt that bleeding is likely to be from a polyp, a rabbi should be consulted, as the woman may not be a *niddah*. Some authorities feel that uterine polyps cause local hormonal changes and thus rule that blood attributed to a polyp or fibroid and to their removal would make her *niddah*.[4]

Malignant lesions

Cancers of the cervix, endometrium, fallopian tubes, or ovaries can present themselves as abnormal bleeding. This is why it is so important that abnormal bleeding be evaluated by a physician, in addition to dealing with the *niddah* problems that may arise. This advice is important for women of all ages. Cancer of the cervix is most common in young women; this is also why Pap smears are so important. In older women, bleeding after a long interval without a period (not due to pregnancy) is particularly suspicious. Twenty five percent of uterine bleeding in post menopausal women is due to reproductive tract cancer.[5] Therefore, abnormal uterine bleeding should always be evaluated.

Complications of pregnancy

Unexplained bleeding in a woman of reproductive age needs to be considered a complication of pregnancy until proven otherwise. The reason is that some causes of pregnancy-related bleeding, such as ectopic pregnancy, are potentially life threatening. Therefore, in almost all situations a preg-

---

[3] Spellacy W.N. "Uterine Leiomyoma" in *Danforth Obstetrics and Gynecology (8th edition)* Philiedlphia: Lippincott Williams and Wilkins, 1998.

[4] Brander K. "Gynecological Procedures and Their Interface with Halacha." *Journal of Halacha and Contemporary Society* 2001; 42:31–45.

[5] March C.M. "Bleeding Problems and Treatment." *Clinical Obstetrics and Gynecology* 1998; 41:928–939.

nancy test should be done to rule out this possibility. This includes women using birth control, as no method is 100% effective. This further includes women who have their monthly periods, as bleeding during pregnancy can be confused with a period. This advice is particularly true when there is any pain together with the bleeding. Most bleeding during pregnancy, if it does not meet the criteria for a permitted stain (less than a *gris*, no halachically relevant sensation, etc.), would render a woman a *niddah*.

Outside causes that affect the reproductive tract

Both systemic diseases that cause problems with coagulation and medications that affect coagulation can cause abnormal bleeding. These generally present themselves as excessive bleeding during menstruation rather than bleeding outside the anticipated time. Thyroid disease can also involve abnormalities of the menstrual cycle.

Dysfunctional uterine bleeding

Dysfunctional uterine bleeding is defined as abnormal uterine bleeding with no demonstrable cause. It is most common at the extremes of the reproductive years (adolescence and peri-menopause) when periods without ovulation are most common. It is so diagnosed after other causes, outlined above, have been ruled out. It results from the hormonal events surrounding the menstrual cycle that occur with aging or anovulatory cycles. Treatment generally consists of hormonal treatments or non-steroidal anti-inflammatory drugs tailored to the woman's age, severity of bleeding, and desire for future children.[6] The progesterone containing IUD is sometimes used for this indication as well.[7] In severe cases, surgical procedures are sometimes needed. These include dilatation and curettage, various forms of endometrial ablation or hysterectomy.[8]

---

[6] March C.M. "Bleeding Problems and Treatment." *Clinical Obstetrics and Gynecology* 1998; 41:928–939.

[7] See Part Four, chapter 3 for more details on this device.

[8] See Part Four, chapter 6 for further details on these methods.

Post-coital bleeding

Bleeding during or immediately after intercourse can be from a number of medical conditions, including irritation of the vagina and cervix. From a halachic standpoint it is important to determine the cause, because of the laws pertaining to רואה מחמת תשמיש ("seeing due to intercourse"). These laws state that if a woman sees blood three times in a row due to intercourse (after going to the *mikveh* each time), she would be forbidden to her husband permanently. Thus, if the bleeding occurs during intercourse and if the bleeding cannot be attributed to other causes such as injury, already after the first occurrence a medical exam should be done to find a cause. After the medical exam she should consult with a rabbi as to how to proceed.[9]

---

[9] There are those that recommend that all couples establish that the woman has a *chazakah* <u>not</u> to see blood due to intercourse. This is established by both the husband and wife wiping the genital area with examination cloths immediately after intercourse, three times in a row. In order for this to be valid, this has to be done three times in a row during the part of her cycle where she sometimes gets her period, although of course not on a day when intercourse is forbidden. It is often difficult to put this into practice. It is <u>necessary</u> to do this if she has actually had post-coital bleeding. See *Igrot Moshe* YD 2:75.

CHAPTER 5

THERAPEUTIC MEDICAL PROCEDURES

Endometrial Ablation

A number of procedures have been developed to remove or destroy the uterine lining without removing the entire uterus. Collectively they are known as endometrial ablation. Methods used include microwave, electrical cautery, laser and thermal balloon. They are meant for women who are not planning further childbearing. In the majority of cases they produce either amenorrhea or markedly reduced bleeding.[1]

Some methods are done with a hysteroscope. One would need to ask the size of the scope used to see if the dilation would render her *niddah* even in the absence of bleeding. Others (such as a hot water balloon) are done via a small catheter. While the bleeding that might be caused by these procedures should logically be considered *dam makkah*, there are those who maintain that total removal of the uterine lining might have a different halachic status. Therefore a woman undergoing these procedures should ask for an individual *psak*.

Dilatation and Curettage (D&C)

In this procedure, the cervical opening is dilated and then the uterine lining is scraped out. This procedure is used as a method of performing first trimester abortions, removing remains after miscarriages and as a treatment method for excessive uterine bleeding.

The currettage definitely produces bleeding. Once again, while this bleeding is logically *dam makkah,* some authorities maintain that removing endometrial lining should be treated as *dam niddah.* An individual question should be asked. Furthermore, if performed after childbirth, then the laws of *yoledet* apply. If performed after a miscarriage or to induce an abortion, she would be either *niddah* or *yoledet* as explained below. If performed not in

---

[1] Lethaby A., Hickey M. "Endometrial Destruction Techniques for Heavy Menstrual Bleeding: A Cochrane Review." *Human Reproduction* 2002; 17:2795–806.

relation to pregnancy, then she might still become *niddah* if the dilation is greater than the amount that would make her *niddah*. In an actual case, a woman should ask the degree of dilation and consult with a rabbi as to how to proceed.

Hysterectomy

This is the complete removal of the uterus. The indications are dysfunctional uterine bleeding that cannot be controlled by other methods, cancer or precancerous lesions of the uterus, severe prolapse of the uterus and, in extreme cases, to prevent death from post-partum hemorrhage. It can be done either via the abdomen or the vagina. Because the only sign of ovarian cancer is irregular bleeding, which a woman without a uterus will not have, sometimes the ovaries are removed at the same time. Since this causes an abrupt menopause unless hormone replacement therapy is given, there are cases, especially with younger women, where the ovaries are left intact.

Removal of the uterus involves the question of the permissibility of permanent sterilization of women.[2] Sterilization is a serious halachic concern as discussed in the section on birth control (p. 162). The level of seriousness is lower for women, according to most opinions. For medical indications it would be permitted, but should not be undertaken simply as a method of birth control.[3] Marital relations after hysterectomy do not constitute הוצאת שכבת זרע לבטלה, "wasting of seed."[4]

After the procedure the woman will probably need to go to the *mikveh* one last time, because of the probably uterine bleeding at the time of the surgery. If all of the uterus has been removed, according to most opinions she will never be a *niddah* again.[5]

---

[2] Endometrial ablation may also raise this concern. However, as it is a relatively new technology, this has not yet been discussed in written halachic sources to the best of my knowledge. Furthermore, there have been rare cases of pregnancy despite that procedure.

[3] Hershler M. "*Hotzaat Evrei Haholadah Be-ishah.*" *Halacha Ve-Refuah* (Jerusalem: Machon Regensburg, 5740).

[4] *Yabia Omer* Part 3 EH 4.

[5] If the uterus is not totally removed (subtotal hysterectomy), then she can still become *niddah*. Thus it is important for a woman to understand the exact proce-

Abortion[6]

Judaism values life, even the potential life of a fetus. Therefore, abortion is generally frowned on in halacha. However, there are rare situations, such as to save the life of the mother, where it will be permitted. As the fetus is considered to be "mere water" prior to 40 days after conception (presumed to be the night of immersing in the *mikveh)*, abortion prior to seven weeks is easier to permit.[7] In cases of severe maternal illness or great distress to the family, later abortions are sometimes permitted. Advice should be sought from a rabbi with expertise in this area. Should a woman undergo an abortion prior to 40 days after conception, she has to follow the laws that apply to a *niddah*. After 40 days the rules of *yoledet* apply.

---

dure that is going to be performed and to discuss it with the surgeon after the procedure to assure that technical difficulties did not lead to a change in plans.

[6] For further reading see: 1) J.D. Bleich. *Contemporary Halachic Problems Vol I* (NY: Ktav, 1977) pp. 325–371. 2) Yosef O. *"Hafsakat Haherayon Leor Hahalacha." Sefer Assia* 1 (Jerusalem: Machon Schlesinger, 1983).

[7] Henkin Y.H. *"Hapalah Kodem Arbaim Yom." Assia* 5757; 15:133–45.

CHAPTER 6

MARITAL RELATIONS

Halachic aspects of marital relations

While much has been written of the Jewish attitude towards sex, little has been written of the specific commandments, and even less about halachic implications of sexual problems.[1] This is partially because it is a topic in which modesty, even verbal modesty, is required. This section is included not to make light of the importance of modesty in this area, but because of a need for some discussion of this topic to prevent couples from suffering needlessly.

Sex is a natural but learned behavior (see Appendix C, pp. 200–204, for further discussion of physiology). For a couple in which neither has prior sexual experience, learning together is part of the bonding process of their marriage. This can take time and should be approached with patience, understanding, and a bit of a sense of humor by both husband and wife. When one member of the couple has prior experience, even more understanding and patience is sometimes needed. It should be remembered that, particularly for those who have had no physical contact prior to marriage, it is sometimes quite an adjustment to make all at once.

---

[1] Steinberg A. "*Hashkafat hayahadut al hachaim haminiim.*" *Sefer Assia* 4 (Jerusalem: Machon Schlesinger, 1983).

The halachic obligation

אִם אַחֶרֶת יִקַּח לוֹ שְׁאֵרָהּ כְּסוּתָהּ וְעֹנָתָהּ לֹא יִגְרָע. (שמות כא:י)

Marital relations are considered one of three biblical obligations that a husband has to his wife. This commandment is known as *onah* or "her time." The exact frequency depends on his profession and the resulting anticipated amount of time spent at home, among other factors. Marital relations are due her on her *mikveh* night and before leaving for a trip, assuming she is not a *niddah*.[2] At other times when she is not a *niddah* they are permitted whenever mutually desired. Marital relations are viewed as part of the way that couples become closer to each other and are an integral part of a marriage. However, it should not be the only focus of a marriage, and sex should not be a constant preoccupation of the husband and wife.[3]

When are they forbidden

In addition to the time when she is a *niddah*, when all physical contact is prohibited, and the days of her anticipated menses when intercourse is forbidden, there are other times when marital relations are forbidden. They are forbidden as a sign of mourning during the week of mourning (*shiva*) of either the husband or wife, and on Tisha B'Av. On Yom Kippur, they are proscribed as one of the five deprivations[4] of the day. In these cases, hugging and kissing are forbidden as well. Whether one needs to keep the added restrictions (the *harchakot*) is a matter of dispute. One should consult with one's own rabbi.

---

[2] *Shulchan Aruch* OH 240.

[3] *Berachot* 22a.

[4] The other four are eating, drinking, wearing leather shoes and annointing with oil.

What is permissible?

There is lots of latitude within halacha as to what is permissible within marital relations.[5] A few principles are inviolable – only with one's spouse, not while the wife is a *niddah*, and only in private.[6] It also has to be mutually acceptable – Judaism does not permit marital rape.

There is other recommended behavior. One such behavior is that intercourse not take place in artificial light or daylight.[7] The reason given in the traditional sources is that inspection in full light might lead to finding something unattractive. Rather than enhance sexual function, fear of unattractiveness may inhibit it, simply because many women are self conscious. Some sources also proscribe looking directly at the vagina.[8] Following this recommendation also assures that women will not feel demeaned by the focused gaze but rather feel that her husband is making love to the total "her" and not to a particular body part.

It is recommended that the couple face each other. Looking at each other helps to ensure that they are concentrating on their relationship and not on anything else.[9]

What if physical relations do not seem to be going right

Even after the couple has learned the basics there are times that physical relations will not go as smoothly as possible. Should the problem persist it is important that the issue be addressed. Further discussion of sexual difficulties and female sexual pain disorders are found in Appendix C (pp. 204–206). A few common problems that men experience are outlined below:

Premature ejaculation is involuntary emission of semen prior to intercourse, or immediately upon the beginning of intercourse. It happens to most men from time to time. If it is chronic, it requires treatment to allow

---

[5] *Shulchan Aruch* EH 25:1 and the gloss of the *Rema* on EH 25:2.

[6] *Shulchan Aruch* EH 25:4.

[7] *Shulchan Aruch* OC 240:11.

[8] *Kallah* 1:9, *Tur* OC 240.

[9] *Shulchan Aruch* OC 240:2.

for pregnancy, as well as due to the halachic concern of wasting seed. Consultation with a urologist or sex therapist should be sought.

Erectile dysfunction is the inability to achieve or maintain erection, commonly known as impotence. At one time this was felt to be mostly psychological, but today it is believed that most cases are physical in origin. Erection requires the interplay of the mind, blood vessels, and nerves. Fatigue or emotional stress can be the cause if it happens occasionally. If the problem persists, a medical condition should be suspected, as many diseases of blood vessels or nerves such as diabetes, hypertension, etc. can lead to this condition. Effective treatments are available. Therefore, medical consultation should be sought.

There is nothing inherently halachically wrong with treating sexual dysfunction. Quite the opposite, it is crucial for the health or survival of the marriage. The question concerns the methods that are often employed. Masturbation is contraindicated by halacha, and staring at the genital area is problematic as well. Therefore, it is important to use a therapist who is sensitive to these concerns and to the laws of *niddah* and is willing to work around them. For example, many sexual therapy techniques involve touch. This would have to be scheduled around the time the couple is permitted to touch and be forbidden when the wife is *niddah*. All these types of issues can be overcome with a sensitive therapist who is willing to work with the couple and rabbinic consultation.

APPENDICES

Appendix A: Review of Physiology of Menstruation and Pregnancy

Appendix B: Taking Care of Oneself During and After Pregnancy

Appendix C: Sexual Anatomy and Physiology

Appendix D: *Mikveh* Construction

Appendix E: Checklist Prior to *Mikveh* Immersion

Appendix F: *Veset* Calendar

Appendix G: The Marriage Contract

Appendix H: What are the Issues Involved in a Married Woman
     Covering her Hair

Appendix I: Authorities Cited and Their Works Relevant to
     Hilchot Niddah

Appendix A

Review of Physiology of Menstruation and Pregnancy

The menstrual cycle is an orderly series of hormonally mediated events that, in the absence of conception, end with the shedding of the uterine lining. Classically, this is pictured as a twenty-eight day cycle, with day one being the first day of bleeding and day twenty-eight being the day prior to the beginning of bleeding of the next cycle. While twenty-eight days is the example generally used, as it divides into an orderly four weeks, anything between 21–35 days is considered normal.

During the first half of the cycle, the lining is shed and then starts to build up again. While the lining is building up, follicles in the ovaries are maturing. Thus this is known as the follicular phase. Approximately mid-cycle (day 14 in our illustrative cycle) the dominant follicle bursts, releasing an ovum or egg. This is known as ovulation. The cells of the follicle that surrounded the ovum at this point are known as the corpus luteum (or "yellow body," due to their appearance under the microscope) and continue to secrete hormones. This half of the cycle is known as the luteal phase.

Pituitary hormones, under the pulsatile stimulation of hormones from hypothalamus, regulate the process. One, known as follicle stimulating hormone (FSH), as its name indicates, leads to the growth of the follicle, and its influence is greater in the first half of the cycle. The second, known as luteinizing hormone (LH), is involved in the formation of the corpus luteum. LH levels rise about twenty-four hours prior to ovulation. This LH surge is what is detected in kits that determine the time of ovulation.

Estrogen is low at the beginning of the cycle, which is why there is often vaginal dryness at the time of the *hefsek taharah*. It continues to rise to mid-cycle, when it has a slight dip around the time of ovulation but is still high. This is experienced by women as increasing vaginal lubrication and secretions. Cervical discharge goes from being thick and sticky to thin and watery. This is one of the signs used to determine that ovulation has taken place. Under the influence of estrogen there is build-up of the uterine lining. Progesterone rises in the second half of the cycle, as it is secreted by the corpus luteum. The fall in progesterone with the involution of the corpus luteum in the absence of fertilization leads to failure to support the uterine lining. This leads to the shedding of the lining and hence to menses.

When the ovum, which is smaller than the size of a pencil dot, is released from the ovary, it is swept up into the fallopian tube. It remains alive for up to 24 hours, after which it disintegrates and is either reabsorbed by the body or expelled as part of the menstrual flow. If during the time it is alive it encounters viable sperm and one sperm penetrates into the egg cell, conception will generally result. Sperm are expelled by the husband as part of the ejaculate during intercourse. They are aided in remaining alive and swimming from the vagina to the fallopian tube by the type of cervical fluid that is secreted by the wife around the time of ovulation. For pregnancy to occur, the meeting usually takes place in the outer third of the fallopian tube.

The fertilized egg, now known as a zygote, continues its path from the fallopian tube to the uterus. Simultaneously it continues to divide and then is referred to as an embryo. When it reaches the uterus, it burrows into the lining (the endometrium). This is known as implantation. Once this happens, it begins to secrete a hormone known as human chorionic gonadotropin (HCG) which signals the corpus luteum to stay alive longer than its usual 14–16 days and to continue to secrete progesterone and thus help maintain the uterine lining. This hormone is what is tested for in pregnancy tests. False negative tests are often the result of doing the test too early. Therefore, if one thinks one is pregnant and has a negative test, it should be repeated a week later.

The embryo continues to develop in the uterus, with groups of cells taking on specific roles (e.g., brain cells, muscle cells) in a process called differentiation. A placenta is also developed which takes over producing the hormones needed to maintain the uterine lining and provides nutrients and oxygen. After about 8 weeks, organs can be identified and the embryo is known as a fetus. This continues to develop for a total of about 38 weeks calculated from the time of conception when, due to signals that are not completely understood, a new hormonal cascade begins, and labor and childbirth takes place.

Appendix B

Taking Care of Oneself During and After Pregnancy

by Talli Y. Rosenbaum, PT[1]

A Jewish woman's transition to marriage and motherhood is marked by a significant change of status, socially as well as halachically. A Jewish woman's life changes drastically when she weds and takes upon herself the study and performance of rituals related to *taharat hamishpachah*, and other *mitzvot* pertinent to her new role. Many Jewish sources deal with the spiritual, social, psychological, and halachic implications of becoming a wife and mother.

However, few sources help prepare women for the significant physical changes a woman undergoes upon marriage. Preparing for the initial *tevilah* in a *mikveh*, immersion and intimacy, as well as the years of pregnancies, births and raising children, when physical fitness and stamina become crucial.

The laws of *tzniut* govern Jewish women to dress and act in a modest fashion. In many circles, spurred by the modern world's enthusiastic approach to physical fitness and coupled with the Jewish adage *"Ushmartem me'od lenafshotechem,"* appropriate women's-only venues for exercise, swim and dance are now encouraged. Physical fitness promotes good health and a strong body. It has emotional benefits as well, by decreasing stress and increasing endorphins, the body's own natural morphine-like "feel good" substance. Physical fitness also improves body image. A woman with a

---

[1] Talli Y. Rosenbaum is a private practice physical therapist, researcher and lecturer, specializing in urogynecological and pelvic floor rehabilitation and an AASECT (American Association of Sex Educators, Counselors and Therapists) certified sexuality counselor. She recently co-founded the Institute for Marital Enrichment which provides sexual education and therapy for Orthodox couples in Israel. She has offices in Tel Aviv, Jerusalem, and Beit Shemesh, Israel. Her website is www.physioforwomen.com.

positive, healthy body image is better equipped to be comfortable with and enjoy physical intimacy, as well as deal with the bodily changes which she will experience throughout the life cycle, and particularly, in her childbearing years.

Pregnancy

The physiologic changes that occur during pregnancy affect nearly every system of the body. Changes in the renal, neurological, cardiovascular, respiratory and endocrine systems, all contribute to creating optimal conditions for carrying and giving birth to a baby. While most changes that occur are not within our control, exercise, proper nutrition, reducing stress and getting enough rest will improve the way we look and feel.

Each pregnancy, labor and delivery, takes a physical toll. During pregnancy, weight gain as well as ligament weakness caused by hormonal changes combine to create a situation whereby it is difficult to maintain optimal posture. Increased breast weight contributes to forward sloping shoulders. Increased abdominal weight can cause the lower back to arch and increase pelvic floor pressure. Because of muscle and ligament weakness and edema, which can cause pressure on various nerves, it is not uncommon to suffer from sciatic type pain, tingling in the arms or pain at the pubic bones. Weakness of the abdominal and pelvic floor muscles during pregnancy, combined with the stress these muscles undergo during delivery, contribute to such problems as chronic lower back pain, prolapse (dropping downward) of the pelvic organs, including the bladder and uterus, and urinary stress incontinence, which is characterized by leakage of small amounts of urine with coughing, laughing, sneezing or impact, such as dancing.

Exercise during pregnancy has numerous benefits. Women who exercise have a decreased risk of gestational diabetes, better stamina during delivery and recover faster. Some studies have linked exercise during pregnancy to fewer interventions during delivery, lower maternal weight gain, decreased body fat and improved muscle tone. This is particularly important for prevention of back pain and other discomforts mentioned above.

The following recommendations follow the 2002 American College of Obstetricians and Gynecologists (ACOG) guidelines for exercise during pregnancy and the postpartum period (*Obstetrics and Gynecology* 2002; 99:171–3).

If you are new to exercise, start slowly. You may want to begin by taking a moderately brisk walk for 15–20 minutes three times a week. If you were exercising regularly before your pregnancy, you may find that you need to make only a few modifications to your regimen. Look for an approved prenatal exercise class. If you cannot find an exercise class in your area designed specifically for pregnancy, you will need to devise your own routine. Every workout session should begin with an adequate warm-up period lasting 5 to 7 minutes to prepare your body for exercise. You can then move into the aerobic portion of your workout, which may include walking, jogging (as long as you can jog comfortably), biking, swimming, tennis and/or a low-impact or step aerobics class. You should plan for 20 to 30 minutes of aerobic activity to maximize the benefits to your cardiovascular system. Keep your heart rate under 150 beats per minute if you are between 20–30 years old, and under 140 bpm if you are 30–40. At the end of the aerobic segment, cool down for at least five minutes by continuing to move slowly and rhythmically. Be sure to hydrate your body by drinking plenty of water. Keep the following guidelines in mind:

– Regular exercise is preferable to sporadic activity. The ideal to strive for is 30 minutes or more of cumulative moderate exercise each day, at least most, if not all, days of the week.

– Avoid exercise in the supine or back-lying position after the first three months of pregnancy.

– Avoid prolonged periods of motionless standing.

– Listen to your body while exercising (if something is painful or causes dizziness, <u>don't</u> do it!)

– <u>Don't</u> exercise to the point of exhaustion.

– Be aware of your changing center of gravity and <u>don't</u> do any type of exercise involving the potential for even mild abdominal trauma.

– Increase your caloric intake to compensate for the additional calories needed for a healthy pregnancy.

– Drink plenty of water before, during and after exercise to regulate your body temperature and that of your baby.

– Resume prepregnancy exercise routines gradually, since many of the physical changes of pregnancy persist 4 to 6 weeks after delivery.

Stop exercising and call your physician if you experience any of the following during exercise: chest pain, vaginal bleeding or any unexplained excess fluid from the vagina, headaches, dizziness, fainting, extreme nausea and/or vomiting, a sudden increase in heart rate or blood pressure that persists after exercise, cessation of perspiration along with nausea and clamminess, sudden swelling of ankles, hands and face, persistent contractions that may suggest premature labor, unusual abdominal pain, swelling, pain and redness in the calf on one leg (phlebitis). In the following conditions, exercise may be contraindicated:

* Pregnancy induced hypertension

* Pre-term rupture of membranes, pre-term labor during the prior or current pregnancy or both

* Incompetent cervix/cerclage

* Persistent second or third trimester bleeding

* Intrauterine growth retardation

* Multiple gestation

In addition, women with certain other medical or obstetric conditions, including chronic hypertension or active thyroid, cardiac, vascular or pulmonary disease, should be evaluated carefully in order to determine whether an exercise program is appropriate.

Postpartum Fitness

The period after giving birth is joyous, but very stressful, physically and emotionally. New mothers, tired from lack of sleep and round the clock feedings, must cope with the feelings associated with becoming a mother, and with subsequent births, the attempt to distribute time and attention to other children as well. Weakness of the muscles stretched out from pregnancy, along with the physical effort of nursing and caring for a baby, can also lead to various aches and pains.

While it is well known that exercise improves fitness, finding the time and energy to exercise in the weeks and months following childbirth is often a challenge in itself. Additionally, many women, particularly those who have been sedentary, are rightfully wary of beginning a program and feel overwhelmed with the prospect of even trying to get back in shape. On the other hand, some women are overly zealous in their quest to get their old bodies back and injure themselves in the process.

The guidelines for exercise after childbirth vary and each woman should discuss when it is appropriate to return to exercise with her obstetrician or midwife. Women who have had a C-section, have been on bed rest, have specific pain problems, or simply don't know where to begin with an exercise program, should ask their obstetrician or midwife for a referral to a physical therapist for a fitness assessment and instruction.

For women who are anxious to return to exercise, it is important to be aware of the changes that the body has undergone. Certain muscles, particularly the abdomen and pelvic floor, are particularly weak after childbirth. Pelvic floor exercises, known as "kegels," are effective in strengthening the pelvic floor muscles and preventing and treating stress incontinence, a condition described by leaking or loss of urine with coughing, laughing, or sneezing. This is actually a quite common (though rarely discussed) condition amongst women in their child-bearing years, and it can worsen later in life if not addressed.

Another not so well known but common fitness consideration that women should be aware of when attempting to strengthen the abdomen is the presence of diastestis rectus. This is defined as a separation of the linea alba which is the soft tissue that connects the two sides of the outermost abdominal muscle. When the abdomen muscles stretch, this tissue can actually separate or tear, and in some cases a bulge can be seen. In severe cases, actual herniation of the internal organs can occur, although this is uncommon. Doing abdominal exercises improperly or too vigorously can increase a diastasis, but certain specific exercises can help correct the problem. Women who suspect that they have this problem may benefit from a consultation with a physical therapist. Although most women are interested in strengthening the abdomen for aesthetic reasons, strong muscles are actually important for maintaining good posture and preventing back pain, as the abdominal muscles help to stabilize the pelvis and lower back.

Other recommendations are as follows:

* Nursing mothers should drink plenty of fluids and wear a sports bra during exercise. For wear at other times, nursing bras should be chosen that offer optimum support.

* Heavy bleeding or bright red blood indicates the need for more recovery time.

* Hormonal imbalances may still be present and women should be aware of joint laxity (looseness).

* Listen to your body. Exercises should be performed to relieve stress, not to add to it.

* Be creative. If time and child-care is a consideration, try and fit exercise in with your daily activities. Put the baby in the stroller and walk rather than drive to the store. Do your kegels (exercises to strengthen pelvic floor muscles) while reading to your children or preparing dinner.

In conclusion, it is important to remember that it is crucial to eat properly and maintain good nutrition. Exercise will help improve strength, mobility, energy and overall fitness, and ultimately afford the postpartum woman with better body awareness, improved self-esteem, and most importantly, better health. As the Rambam writes in *Hilchot Deot* 4:1, "A whole and healthy body is one of the ways of *Hashem*."

Appendix C

Sexual Anatomy and Physiology

by Talli Y. Rosenbaum, PT[1]

Sexual activity between a husband and wife is the legitimate act of expressing love and intimacy in a physical manner. It is a *mitzvah* not only for the sake of procreation, but for fulfilling the mitzvah of *onah*, providing one's wife with physical pleasure and satisfaction. Sexual activity, while considered "natural," takes place due to a complex combination of physiological and emotional factors. And while sexual arousal is indeed a natural inclination when a husband and wife are attracted to each other, sexual behavior is a learning process, during which the intimacy between a couple is strengthened.

This learning process requires a combination of patience, a sense of humor, some basic sex education and the actual belief that the intense physical pleasures are not only permissible, but desirable. Sexual activity is intensely physical, but fraught with powerful emotions, particularly for the recently married young couple. Therefore, while some couples eagerly await the wedding night and easily consummate their marriage, others need some time to adjust to expressing physical affection before sexual intercourse is attempted. While many religious couples are well prepared and well versed in the *halachot* relating to *taharat hamishpachah*, many are often not adequately informed as to the basics of sexuality. In fact, little information has been

---

[1] Talli Y. Rosenbaum is a private practice physical therapist, researcher and lecturer, specializing in urogynecological and pelvic floor rehabilitation and an AASECT (American Association of Sex Educators, Counselors and Therapists) certified sexuality counselor. She recently co-founded the Institute for Marital Enrichment which provides sexual education and therapy for Orthodox couples in Israel. She has offices in Tel Aviv, Jerusalem, and Beit Shemesh, Israel. Her website is www.physioforwomen.com.

published specifically for Jewish religious couples regarding basic facts of sex education, including genital anatomy, the physiology of the sexual response, and how to deal with potential sexual problems. This text will attempt to clarify these issues.

Female Anatomy and Physiology

External

The *vulva* is the entire visible genital area, from the area of the pubic hair down to the anus. What is visible externally, are the *perineum, labia, urethra,* and *clitoris.*

The *perineum* is the area that connects the anus to the vagina. It is a hairless area of skin, which often tears or is intentionally cut during child-birth, in a procedure known as an episiotomy.

The *labia* are the flaps of tissue that fold together over the vagina. The *outer labia* are generally covered with hair, and the inner labia are smooth and rich in blood supply. The labia have sensory nerve endings which are sensitive to touch and are a source of sexual stimulation.

Inside the folds of the labia, above the entrance to the vagina, lies the *urethra,* a small opening for the passage of urine. Above that is the *clitoris,* the most sensitive area of a woman's genitals. The clitoris is normally obstructed by a hood, and it becomes exposed during sexual stimulation. The clitoris' function is to provide sexual pleasure, and with stimulation there is increased blood flow to the clitoris which enlarges, and becomes erect.

Internal

Just inside the inner lips, is the opening to the *vagina.* Prior to the first episode of sexual intercourse, the vagina is often, but not always, partially obstructed by a thin membranous layer known as the *hymen.* There are many misconceptions related to the presence of the hymen as proof of a woman's virginity. In fact, there are sexually active women who have hymenal tissue, while some virgins do not. This is because the hymen can be stretched or torn by physical activity, or tampon use. If an intact hymen is penetrated in an aggressive fashion, there can be large amounts of bleeding. If, however, the wife is aroused, lubricated, and relaxed, penetration can occur with minimal trauma to the hymen and often little or no bleeding.

The vagina is tube shaped and about 6 inches in length. At the tip of the vagina is the *cervix,* which opens to the *uterus.* Women who have not been sexually active, and have not used tampons, may have difficulty with initial insertion, even of a *bedikah* cloth. It is important to note that while the vagina may appear narrow, it has the amazing capacity to expand (as during childbirth) and contract.

Lying directly inside the opening to the vagina are muscles known as the *pelvic floor muscles.* By learning how to contract and then relax these muscles, most women can master painless penetration of *bedikah* cloths and tampons. It is recommended that a few weeks before the wedding night, women take the time, perhaps while relaxing in the bathtub, to get to know their own anatomy. They should try and insert a finger or two into the vagina, and learn to contract and relax the internal muscles. This will allow a more relaxed and comfortable initial sexual experience.

Male Anatomy and Physiology

In males, the penis is generally the most sensitive area. The *scrotum* is the pouch below. The *scrotum* houses the *testicles* where sperm is produced. Mature sperm cells travel from there to the epididymus which lies on top of the testicles. The head or *glans* of the penis houses the urethra, the opening where urine and semen pass. There are tubes of spongy tissue inside the penis known as *corpus cavernosa.* With sexual arousal this tissue fills with blood and causes the penis to become erect. During ejaculation, rhythmic contractions cause the sperm to travel through the *prostate gland* and *seminal vesicles* where secretions rich in nutrients combine with them to form *semen* which is expelled through the urethra.

The Physiology of Sexual Function

Sexual intercourse is the insertion of the penis into the vagina. Sexual function is generally divided into four stages: *desire, arousal, orgasm* and *resolution. Desire* for sex occurs due to both physiological, emotional, and situational factors. It is a normal condition, governed by hormones, and influenced by outside factors, such as stress and relationship issues. At certain times, such as during the postpartum period, hormonal changes combined with fatigue and stress contribute to decreased sexual desire. It is important to be aware that this is a natural phenomenon, and not necessarily an indication of marital difficulties. Many women report sexual desire peaks at various times throughout the cycle. Fortunately for some women, these peaks often correspond with the week prior to the menses, and around ovulation; however, women vary as to when they feel the most sexual desire.

Sexual Arousal is a sensual feeling of warmth and pleasure, during which physiological changes occur that cause the body to be receptive to sex. In females there is increased blood flow to the labia, vagina, and clitoris. The vagina shortens and widens in preparation for intercourse. Glands in the vagina secrete fluid to moisten and lubricate the vaginal walls, facilitating easier penetration. There is a rising up of the cervix, ovaries, and fallopian tubes, preventing the pelvic pain with intercourse that is likely to occur when intercourse takes place in the absence of arousal. In males, the corpus spongeosum fills with blood leading to erection of the penis.

Orgasm is considered the peak of sexual pleasure. During orgasm there is an increase in the heart rate and breathing. In women, there are rhythmical contractions of the vaginal and pelvic floor muscles. Often a small amount of fluid (known as female ejaculate) is released from the urethra. In males, there are rhythmic contractions leading to ejaculation of semen. It is important to be aware that research has indicated that while some women do reach orgasm during intercourse itself, the majority of women reach orgasm only through direct stimulation of the clitoris. Therefore, a couple should not worry if they don't reach this stage simultaneously. Similarly a couple should not worry if a woman does not reach orgasm every time. In the process of an act of intercourse that includes ejaculation, a male will experience orgasm. Women, on the other hand, can experience this act without orgasm. Therefore, it may take time for some women to begin having orgasms. Indeed, what strengthens the bond of intimacy between a couple is learning what is mutually pleasurable to one another.

Resolution is the final stage, when the body cools down and returns physiologically to normal. The heart rate and breathing decrease, the swelling of organs resolves, and it is a period of feeling calm, relaxed and satisfied. While women are able to continue to be aroused and reach orgasm during this period, men need to complete the resolution process before they are able to become erect again.

Sexual activity may occur in the absence of one or more of these components. For example, a woman returning from the *mikveh* may occasionally feel tired and not particularly full of desire, yet as love making commences, she becomes aroused and completes the cycle. Recent research on female sexuality has indicated that women often don't feel the same desire as men do, but in fact become desirous of sexual activity once they became aroused with physical contact. Sometimes she feels desire, arousal, and excitement, but doesn't always reach orgasm. Occasionally the male may have difficulty sustaining an erection or may ejaculate too soon. These are common situations and most couples will experience them at some point. If, however, these problems are persistent, prevent sexual activity or enjoyment thereof, or cause distress, they are considered "disorders."

Sexual disorders are generally classified as follows:

Hypoactive sexual desire disorder is a condition whereby the man or woman has a complete lack of desire for sex, as well as an absence of thoughts about sex. While emotional factors may be at play, it is a condition which often has a physiologic basis, so it should first be discussed with one's physician. Possible causes include hormonal deficits, certain medications (including hormonal contraceptives) and even certain medical conditions. Included in this category is *sexual aversion disorder*. This occurs when an individual has a distaste for sexual activity and a phobia about touching the sexual organs.

Female Sexual Arousal Disorder is the inability to attain the physiologic response of arousal, such as lubrication, increased blood flow to the vagina and clitoris, and nipple sensitivity.

Orgasmic Disorders (also known as inorgasmia) is the inability to achieve orgasm, even though there is sufficient desire and arousal. It can be primary, meaning a woman has never achieved orgasm, or secondary, often as a result of surgery, trauma, medication or hormone deficiency. Many cases of primary inorgasmia, are actually a result of lack of sex education. In some cases there has been no instruction that women have orgasms, or that stimulation of the clitoris must occur in some manner in order to achieve one.

Sexual Pain Disorders are unfortunately very common and not well understood. While once thought to be completely "in a woman's head" these conditions are now known to have a physiologic basis. *Dyspareunia* is a general term which means "pain with intercourse." Most women experience it at some point, whether due to a yeast or urinary tract infection, or vaginal dryness due to hormonal factors. Once the cause is identified, it is usually easily treated.

Some women suffer with prolonged dyspareunia after childbirth, due to painful stitches from episiotomy or tears. It is important to report this problem to one's physician, as treatment such as physical therapy for this condition is available. When pain with intercourse persists with no clearly identifiable cause, the diagnosis of *vulvar vestibulitis* should be considered. This is a condition whereby there is a persistent pain with touch or penetration at the entrance to the vagina. While some gynecologists treat this with surgery, most women opt for very successfully conservative treatment with physical therapy. This treatment includes increasing blood flow to the vagina and healing the affected area with pelvic floor exercise and *biofeedback,* a computer assisted device which measures muscle activity and teaches women how to contract and properly relax the muscles.

Vaginismus is a condition whereby a woman is unable to allow penetration even when there is an expressed desire to do so, and responds to attempted penetration by retreating and tightening up her vaginal muscles. In additon to not being able to allow intercourse, women with vaginismus don't use tampons and often have a great deal of difficulty inserting *bedikah* cloths as well. This is sometimes due to intense fear or anxiety, a belief that their opening is "too small" or does not exist, and sometimes is a result of another underlying condition, such as a thick and difficult to penetrate hymen, a narrow vaginal canal or presence of vestibulitis. It is treatable by a number of methods that lead to relaxation of the area to allow penetration such as awareness of one's own vulvar and vaginal anatomy, relaxation techniques, pelvic floor muscle exercises and biofeedback. *Vaginismus* can also be treated with vaginal dilators, which are plastic rods of increasing width, meant to slowly stretch the vaginal opening as well as allow the woman to overcome her fear of penetration.

Appendix D

Mikveh Construction[1]

Ritual immersion needs to take place in water that has accumulated natural-ly (not *she'uvim*, or "drawn water"), and in a pool that does not have the halachic status of a *kli* (vessel). A mikveh is based on a minimum of 40 *seah* (approximately 331 liters or 87.5 US gallons[2]) of accumulated rainwater.[3] In practice, one does not immerse directly in the pool of rainwater, but in a pool of tapwater that is directly connected with the rainwater reserves. (*otzrot*). This allows the water used for immersion to be changed for cleanliness, even when new rainwater will not be available.

There are three ways in which the pools can be connected:

1. *Hazraah* (הזרעה) – If there are already 40 *seah* of natural water in a *mikveh*, one can continue to add drawn water without interfering with its status. The added water itself assumes the status of natural water. According to most opinions this can continue ad infinitum. Thus on one side of the pool there is an *otzar hazraah* initially consisting of rainwater. Tap water is added into this pool, which then overflows into the main pool(s) of the *mikveh* where immersion takes place.

---

[1] This is a simple summary of basic principles. Actual rules for construction are far more complicated, and building a *mikveh* should only be undertaken by those with expertise in this matter.

[2] Rav Chaim Naeh, *Sefer Shiurei Torah* 3:29. *Pinchas Even Yerushalayim*, 5707.

[3] In cases of need, large blocks of ice or snow can be melted to fill the rainwater pool, and the water is not considered "drawn."

2. *Hashakah* (השקה) – When a pool of tap water has direct contact ("kisses") the rainwater, the drawn water attains the halachic status of *mikveh* water. Thus, an *otzar hashakah* of rainwater is located next to the immersion pool and connected to it via a small hole in the wall.[4]

3. *Hamshachah* (המשכה) – If drawn water runs along the ground for a certain distance prior to entering the *mikveh*, it is no longer considered drawn. Therefore, the waters of the *otzar hazraah* often run along the ground prior to entering the main pool.

There are advantages and disadvantages to each of these methods. Due to the grave consequences should the *mikveh* not be halachically valid, most *mikvaot* for use by women today are constructed to use all three of these methods and are thus valid according to all opinions. As men's *mikvaot* are used only due to custom, the rules for their construction are more lenient. Therefore, women should not use the men's *mikveh* even when the men are not present.

---

[4] Some *mikvaot* also add an *otzar hashakah* underneath the tap-water pool, following Lubavitch practice. For further discussion of this see: Dichovsky S, Mirveh Y. *"Mikveh al Gabei Mikveh." Techumin* 5751; 11:248–260.

Appendix E

Checklist Prior to *Mikveh* Immersion

1. Is this the correct night?

    a. Did a minimum of five days (for Sephardim, four days) pass from the onset of what made her a *niddah*, prior to beginning the seven blood-free days?

    b. Was a *hefsek taharah* performed?

    c. Did seven blood-free days pass, with the seventh being (at the latest) the day preceding the night of immersion?

2. Have foreign material /barriers been removed?

    a. jewelry,[1] clothes, bandages,[2] contact lenses

    b. dirt, ink, makeup[3]

    c. nails cut[4] or very well cleaned

---

[1] If anything is stuck, such as a ring, ask beforehand what to do.

[2] If something cannot be removed for medical reasons, ask beforehand whether it is still possible to use the *mikveh*.

[3] If difficult to remove and in good condition, ask beforehand.

[4] The custom is to cut nails. If it is difficult to do so for professional or emotional reasons, it is sufficient to have them well-cleaned.

3. *Chafifah* – Generally done by taking a bath, can also be done in the shower.

a. Hair-covered parts of body are washed in warm water.

b. Hair of the head is combed, other hair is separated by hand.

c. Preferably, the entire body is washed in warm water, but if there is a shortage, cold water is acceptable for the rest of the body other than the hair. If not even cold water is readily available, just assure there is no dirt or other foreign matter, and save the water for the places listed below.

4. Folds of body washed preferably with warm water:

a. Underarms[5]

b. Neck folds

c. Folds between thighs

d. Under the breasts

e. Between any folds of fat

5. Hidden places – first three are washed preferably with warm water

a. Clean between the toes

b. Gently clean the navel

c. Clean external vaginal and anal areas

---

[5] If she does not shave her underarms, they are included under *chafifah*.

d. Blow the nose and remove protruding crusts or mucus

e. Clean the external areas of the ear canal[6] and the folds of the ear lobe

f. Brush and floss teeth

Prior to immersion, it is a good idea to use the bathroom. The concern is that if one is straining to "hold it in," one will not allow water to enter the crevices it normally does in the *mikveh*. It is a good idea to do this prior to washing one's body, as then one does not need to re-wash the vaginal or rectal area.

6. Inspection – Inspect the entire body to assure no barriers are left. This should be done just prior to immersing.

a. Check all visible areas by looking

b. Check by touch areas one cannot see[7]

---

[6] Anything deeper than where the finger reaches would be considered "בלוע" ("swallowed"). One does not have to put a cotton tip applicator deep into the canal unless she routinely does this, in which case she would be *makpid*. Doing so, in fact, can cause damage to the ear.

[7] Most *mikvaot* provide a mirror which enables looking at the back, etc. In the absence of this or of adequate light, feeling is sufficient. If, nevertheless, something is discovered on the skin right after immersion, a rabbi should be consulted.

Appendix F – *Veset* Calendar

Hebrew Date	*Onah* (day or night)	Interval from day one of last menses	Associated symptoms (if any)	Date of *veset* next month – date[1]	Date of *veset* next cycle – interval	Date of *veset* next cycle – day 30

[1] The *onot prishah* are calculated according to the Hebrew calendar. However, for those of us who are more aware of the English date than the Hebrew one, it may be helpful to also write the English date.

Appendix G – The Marriage Contract[1]

On the_____ day of the week on the_____ day of the Hebrew month in the year_____ since the traditional date of Creation, following the count that we count here in_____ (the name of the city), [this is witness] how_____ (the name of the groom) said to_____ (the name of the bride), "Be my wife according to the laws of Moshe and Israel. I will worship, treasure, feed and provide for you according to the laws of Jewish men who worship, treasure, feed and truthfully provide for their wives. I will give you the money due to you_____ (200 *zuz* for a wife's first marriage, 100 *zuz* for a succeeding one) following biblical law, and your food, clothes, necessities and conjugal rights." And_____ (the name of the bride) agreed to be his wife. The dowry that she brings from her father's house, whether in silver or in gold, in jewelry or clothing, whether furniture or li- nens;_____ (the name of the groom) assumes responsibility for, in return for 100 *zuz*. And the groom wishes to add another 100 *zuz* for a total of 200 *zuz*. The groom_____ (name of groom) states that "The guarantee of this marriage contract and dowry and supplement, I obligate myself and my heirs after me to pay from all that I own, from all that I have purchased in the past and that I may purchase in the future. All these will be a guarantee and collateral to pay the amount of this marriage contract, this dowry and this sup- plement, even the shirt off my back, in my life and after my life from this day and forever." The amount of the marriage contract, the dowry and the supple- ment_____ (name of the groom) accepts as the marriage contract and the supplements that are customary among the women of Israel that are done according to the decrees of the Sages, of blessed memory, as a binding contract and not as a mere formula. And_____ (the name of the groom) gives this to the bride, all that is written and explained above in usable currency, and it is all valid and properly executed.

_____ (Signature of witness one)

_____ (Signature of witness two)

---

[1] There are a number of slightly different versions.

Appendix H

Issues Involved in a Married Woman Covering her Hair

While not actually part of the laws of *niddah*, the issue of hair covering is one that is unique to marriage. Therefore a summary of the relevant aspects is provided here.

וּפָרַע אֶת ראשׁ הָאִשָּׁה... לִימֵּד עַל בְּנוֹת יִשְׂרָאֵל שֶׁהֵן מְכַסּוֹת רָאשֵׁיהֶן.
(ספרי במדבר, פיסקא יא)

In a discussion of the procedure of investigating a *sotah* – a woman suspected of adultery[1] – the priest uncovers the woman's hair. The halachic midrash derives from this that, normally, married women's heads are covered.

The Talmud (*Ketuvot* 72a) lists circumstances under which a woman would forfeit the sum of money due to her by her marriage contract (*ketubah*). Among these is "One who transgresses the laws of Moses, or Jewish practice." Examples of the laws of Moses include feeding her husband untithed produce, having relations with him while she is a *niddah*, not removing the mandatory *challah* portion from his bread, and making vows that she does not keep. Among the examples of violations of "Jewish practice" is going out to the market with her head uncovered.

Citing the source-text about the *sotah*, the Talmud asks, is not having her head covered a biblical commandment? It answers that she transgresses the biblical commandment only if her head is completely uncovered. If she has a minimal or defective headcovering, such as a porous basket, she does not transgress the laws of Moses but violates Jewish

---

[1] In order for this procedure to be invoked, the woman first had to be warned not to be alone with a particular man, and do so nevertheless.

practice. The Talmud then discusses different places where the rules of head-covering might be different, such as in a courtyard or passageway.

Another talmudic source (*Berachot* 24a) raises a second aspect of headcovering, that of modesty. The *Shulchan Aruch* (OC 75:2) thus rules that a man cannot say *shema* in front of a woman's hair that is generally covered, due to sexual distraction. (This may be part of the reason that even married women who do not cover their heads in public, often do so in the synagogue.) Due to the fact, much decried in the *poskim*, that many married women have stopped covering their hair, it no longer has the same sexual connotations. Therefore, without condoning the situation, some authorities such as the *Aruch Hashulchan*[2] and Rav Moshe Feinstein[3] rule that *shema* may be recited in such circumstances.[4]

The current reality for over 150 years in Europe and then America is that there are women who keep other aspects of halacha but do not cover their hair. Much has been written about this requirement today. For further study of the halachic issues see:

1. Schiller M. "The Obligation of Married Women to Cover their Hair." *Journal of Halacha and Contemporary Society* (1995) 30: 81–108 and letter to the editor by Michael Broyde in the next issue (1996) 31:123–128.

2. Regev D. "*Yotse'ah ve Roshah Parua.*" *Hamevaser* (1998) 38:18–23, 57–58.

3. Henkin Y. *Understanding Tsniut* (Jerusalem: Urim, 2008), pp. 25–50, 109–112. *Responsa on Contemporary Jewish Women's Issues* (New Jersey: Ktav, 2003) chapter 16. In Hebrew: *Bnei Banim*, Volume III, number 21 and "*Shiur Kisui Rosh Shel Nashim.*" *Techumin* 5753;13:290–8.

---

[2] *Shulchan Aruch* OH 75:7

[3] *Shulchan Aruch* OH 1:42

[4] The *Mishna Brurah* (*Beur Halachah* OH 75:2) continues to prohibit this.

4. Broyde, MJ. "Hair Covering & Jewish Law: Biblical and Objective (*Dat Moshe*) or Rabbinic and Subjective (*Dat Yehudit*)?" Tradition (2009) 42.3:97–179. Shulman EB. "Hair Covering and Jewish Law: A Response." Tradition (2010) 43.2:73–108.

For a collection of essays, primarily by women, grappling with this issue, see: Schreiber L, *Hide and Seek: Jewish Women and Hair Covering* (Jerusalem: Urim Publications, 2003; reissued in softcover in 2006). Personal practice of hair covering should be discussed in depth with one's rabbi.

Appendix I

Authorities Cited and Their Works Relevant to *Hilchot Niddah*

ARUCH HASHULCHAN – compendium by Rabbi Yehiel Michel Epstein (Russia, 1829–1908) that follows the order of the *Shulchan Aruch*.

BADEI HASHULCHAN – commentary on the parts of *Shulchan Aruch* relevant to *hilchot niddah* by Rabbi Feivel Cohen (New York, contemporary).

BNEI BANIM – collection of responsa by Rabbi Yehuda Herzl Henkin (Israel, contemporary). Many include the opinions of his grandfather Rabbi Yosef Eliahu Henkin.

CHATAM SOFER – responsa by Rabbi Moses Sofer (Germany, 1762–1839).

CHAVOT DAAT – commentary on *Shulchan Aruch* by Rabbi Yaakov Lorberbaum (Poland, 1760–1832).

CHAZON ISH – Rabbi Avraham Yeshayah Kareliz (Bnei Brak, 1878–1953).

IGROT MOSHE – collection of responsa by Rabbi Moshe Feinstein (New York 1895–1986).

MISHNAH BRURAH – Rabbi Yisrael Meir Kagan (Poland, 1839–1933). Commentary on *Shulchan Aruch Orach Chaim*. [Rabbi Kagan is also known as the *Chofetz Chaim*, the title of his work on *Lashon Hara*.]

MORDECHAI ELIYAHU – Contemporary *posek* in Israel (1929–2010). Former Sephardic Chief Rabbi. His book *Darchei Taharah* is widely used in Israel to teach brides.

NODA BI-YEHUDAH – collection of responsa by Rabbi Ezekiel ben Judah Landau (Poland 1713–1793) Also authored *Dagul Merevava*, comments on the *Shulchan Aruch*.

OR ZARUA – R. Yitzchak ben R. Moshe of Vienna (c. 1180–c. 1250).

PITCHEI TESHUVAH – work by R. Abraham Zvi Hirsh Eisenstadt (Lithuania, 1813–1868) that summarizes the rulings of hundreds of responsa, organized according to the corresponding sections of the *Shulchan Aruch*.

RAMBAM – Rabbi Moses ben Maimon (Maimonides) (Spain, 1138–Egypt, 1204), authored *Mishneh Torah* (also known as *Yad Ha-Chazakah)*, which summarizes the entire oral law.

RAMBAN – Rabbi Moses ben Nachman (Nachmanides) (Spain, 1194–Israel, 1270).

RASHBA – Rabbi Solomon ben Abraham Aderet (Spain, 1235–1310). His book on *hilchot niddah* is known as *Torat Ha-Bayit*.

RAN – Rabbi Nissim ben Reuven of Gerona (Spain, 1320–1380). his works on *hilchot niddah* are found in his commentary to the code of the *RIF* (Alfasi).

RASHI – Rabbi Solomon Yitzchaki (France, 1040–1105). Wrote essential commentaries to the Bible and Talmud.

RAVAD – Rabbi Abraham ben David (Provence, 1120–1198). Most of his opinions on *hilchot niddah* are found in his book *Baalei Hanefesh* and his glosses to the *Mishna Torah* of the Rambam.

REMA – Rabbi Moses ben Israel Isserles (Poland 1525 (1530?)–1572) – glosses (*hagahot*) to *Shulchan Aruch* which reflected Ashkenazic halachic practice.

RIF – Rabbi Yitzchak Alfasi (Algeria, 1013–Spain, 1103) – author of one of the first codes of Jewish Law which follows the order of the Talmud.

ROSH – Rabbi Asher ben Yechiel (Germany, 1250–Spain, 1327). His rulings on *hilchot niddah* are found in his commentary on the tractate *Niddah* and are brought in the compendium, the *Tur*, written by his son.

SHACH – Rabbi Shabbetai ben Meir Ha-Kohen (Lithuania, 1621–1662)'s *Siftei Kohen* (acronym: *Shach*) is one of the most important commentaries on *Shulchan Aruch Yoreh De'ah*. His *Nekudot Ha-Kesef* is a response to R. David Ha-Levi's commentary on *Yoreh De'ah* (see *Taz*).

SHIUREI SHEVET HALEVI – Rabbi Shmuel Halevi Wosner (Bnei Brak, contemporary). This book, notes from lectures given, is organized according to the *Shulchan Aruch Yoreh Deah*.

SHULCHAN ARUCH – by Rabbi Joseph ben Ephraim Caro (Spain, 1488–Safed, 1575). His main work is the *Bet Yosef*, an encyclopedic commentary on Rabbi Jacob ben Asher's halachic code, the *Tur*. The *Shulchan Aruch* is a concise rendition of Rav Caro's rulings.

TAZ (Turei Zahav) – R. David Ha-Levi's commentary on *Shulchan Aruch Yoreh De'ah*.

TUR (short for *Arba Turim* or four columns) – a halachic work by Rabbi Jacob ben Asher (Spain, 1275–1340, the son of the ROSH) on which the SHULCHAN ARUCH is based.

TZITZ ELIEZER – collection of responsa, with many on issues of medicine and halacha, by Rabbi Eliezer Judah Waldenburg (Israel, contemporary).

YABIA OMER, YECHAVEH DA'AT – collections of responsa by Rabbi Ovadia Yosef (Israel, contemporary), former Sephardic Chief Rabbi of Israel.

INDEX

About the Author

Deena R. Zimmerman MD MPH IBCLC (International Board Certified Lactation Consultant) is a physician with a life-long love for Judaic Studies. She received her BA from Yale University and MD from the Albert Einstein College of Medicine. She completed her pediatric residency, chief residency and Masters in Public Health at the University of Medicine and Dentistry of New Jersey, where she also served on the faculty as Assistant Professor of Clinical Pediatrics for four years. Dr. Deena Zimmerman currently works as a pediatrician for Maccabi Health Services and TEREM-Immediate Medical Care, and is Medical Advisor to the Jerusalem Breastfeeding Center.

One of the first graduates of the Nishmat's Keren Ariel Program as a *Yoetzet Halacha* (Women's Halachic Advisor), Deena has written a number of articles related to women's health issues and Jewish law and lectures extensively on Medicine, Women's Health and Jewish Law and Jewish Medical Ethics. In addition, Deena directs the Nishmat's Women's Health and Halachic websites (www.yoatzot.org and www.jewishwomenshealth.org) for the general public and for healthcare providers. She lives in Israel with her husband Rabbi Sammy Zimmerman and their five children.